Editor
Mary S. Jones, M.A.

Editor in Chief
Karen J. Goldfluss, M.S. Ed.

Creative Director
Karen J. Goldfluss, M.S. Ed.

Cover Artist
Diem Pascarella

Illustrator
Clint McKnight

Art Coordinator
Renée Mc Elwee

Imaging
Leonard P. Swierski

Publisher

Mary D. Smith, M.S. Ed.

Instant Math Practice

Standards-based exercises for year-round practice!

- Number and Operations
- Algebra
- Geometry
- Measurement and Data
- Problem Solving

Teacher Created Resources

CORRELATED TO COMMON CORE STANDARDS

TCR 2554

Author
Damon James

Teacher Created Resources
6421 Industry Way
Westminster, CA 92683
www.teachercreated.com
ISBN: 978-1-4206-2554-7
© 2013 Teacher Created Resources
Made in U.S.A.

Teacher Created Resources

Table of Contents

Table of Contents

Introduction

The *Instant Math Practice* series was written to provide students with frequent opportunities to master and retain important math skills. The unit practice pages are designed to target and reinforce those skills. As students become active learners and discover important mathematical relationships, they are more likely to improve their problem-solving skills and gain a new-found confidence in math. When using this book, take every opportunity possible to incorporate the practice exercises into your current curriculum.

This book addresses a variety of math skills and topics that help students build foundational knowledge in the following areas: numbers and numeration, addition, subtraction, multiplication, division, fractions, decimals, money, geometric shapes, length, area, problem solving, and so much more. In addition, the multiple practice opportunities in each unit facilitate students' mastery of math skills and concepts.

How to Use the Activity Pages

There are over 120 student activity pages, with each page containing six practice sections. The contents of each practice page relate directly to the skills addressed on that page. However, each of the six sections is designed to allow students to practice a skill in different ways. For example, on a page that focuses on place value, students may be asked to represent an expanded number as a numeral, to write a numeral in a chart to show its place value, to express the value of a digit in the given numeral, or to show a number in word form. By offering a variety of ways to practice a math skill on any given page, students think about and learn multiple approaches to mastering that skill.

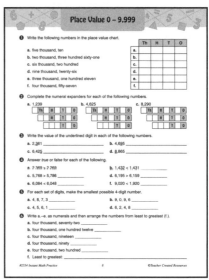

There are several ways in which to use the activities in this book. You may wish to coordinate each unit with whatever math concept is being introduced to the class. The student pages can be used to pre- or post-assess students as well. Practice pages can be assigned as homework or additional class work. An answer key is included in the back of the book.

Common Core State Standards Correlations (CCSS)

Correlations have been provided for the Common Core State Standards for Math. For quick viewing of the math correlations, a chart is provided on pages 5 and 6 of this book. (Note: This version does not contain page titles but does reference the page numbers.) For a printable PDF version of the correlations chart, go to *www.teachercreated.com/standards/*. These charts correlate student page activities to applicable standards within a given domain.

Common Core State Standards Correlation

The student practice pages in *Instant Math Practice* meet one or more of the following Common Core State Standards © Copyright 2010. National Governors Association Center for Best Practices and Council of Chief State School Officers. All rights reserved. For more information about the Common Core State Standards, go to *http://www.corestandards.org/*.

Mathematics Standards	Page
Operations & Algebraic Thinking	
Use the four operations with whole numbers to solve problems.	
4.OA.1. Interpret a multiplication equation as a comparison, e.g., interpret $35 = 5 \times 7$ as a statement that 35 is 5 times as many as 7 and 7 times as many as 5. Represent verbal statements of multiplicative comparisons as multiplication equations.	13, 30, 31, 32, 33, 34, 35, 36, 51, 126
4.OA.2. Multiply or divide to solve word problems involving multiplicative comparison, e.g., by using drawings and equations with a symbol for the unknown number to represent the problem, distinguishing multiplicative comparison from additive comparison.	30, 41, 42, 43, 44, 45, 46, 47, 48, 49, 50
4.OA.3. Solve multistep word problems posed with whole numbers and having whole-number answers using the four operations, including problems in which remainders must be interpreted. Represent these problems using equations with a letter standing for the unknown quantity. Assess the reasonableness of answers using mental computation and estimation strategies including rounding.	23, 24, 47, 48, 49, 126
Gain familiarity with factors and multiples.	
4.OA.4. Find all factor pairs for a whole number in the range 1–100. Recognize that a whole number is a multiple of each of its factors. Determine whether a given whole number in the range 1–100 is a multiple of a given one-digit number. Determine whether a given whole number in the range 1–100 is prime or composite.	38, 39, 40, 45, 49, 50, 52
Generate and analyze patterns.	
4.OA.5. Generate a number or shape pattern that follows a given rule. Identify apparent features of the pattern that were not explicit in the rule itself. *For example, given the rule "Add 3" and the starting number 1, generate terms in the resulting sequence and observe that the terms appear to alternate between odd and even numbers. Explain informally why the numbers will continue to alternate in this way.*	9, 14, 15, 31, 32, 33, 34, 35, 36, 37, 38, 53
Number & Operations in Base Ten	
Generalize place value understanding for multi-digit whole numbers.	
4.NBT.1. Recognize that in a multi-digit whole number, a digit in one place represents ten times what it represents in the place to its right. *For example, recognize that $700 \div 70 = 10$ by applying concepts of place value and division.*	8, 9, 10, 11, 41, 42
4.NBT.2. Read and write multi-digit whole numbers using base-ten numerals, number names, and expanded form. Compare two multi-digit numbers based on meanings of the digits in each place, using >, =, and < symbols to record the results of comparisons.	7, 8, 9, 10, 11, 14, 123, 124
4.NBT.3. Use place value understanding to round multi-digit whole numbers to any place.	10, 22, 29
Use place value understanding and properties of operations to perform multi-digit arithmetic.	
4.NBT.4. Fluently add and subtract multi-digit whole numbers using the standard algorithm.	16, 17, 18, 19, 20, 21, 23, 24, 25, 26, 27, 28, 50, 51, 122, 123, 124, 125
4.NBT.5. Multiply a whole number of up to four digits by a one-digit whole number, and multiply two two-digit numbers, using strategies based on place value and the properties of operations. Illustrate and explain the calculation by using equations, rectangular arrays, and/or area models.	30, 31, 32, 33, 34, 35, 36, 37, 38, 49, 50, 122, 123, 126
4.NBT.6. Find whole-number quotients and remainders with up to four-digit dividends and one-digit divisors, using strategies based on place value, the properties of operations, and/or the relationship between multiplication and division. Illustrate and explain the calculation by using equations, rectangular arrays, and/or area models.	31, 43, 44, 45, 46, 47, 48, 49, 126
Number & Operations - Fractions	
Extend understanding of fraction equivalence and ordering.	
4.NF.1. Explain why a fraction a/b is equivalent to a fraction $(n \times a)/(n \times b)$ by using visual fraction models, with attention to how the number and size of the parts differ even though the two fractions themselves are the same size. Use this principle to recognize and generate equivalent fractions.	51, 56, 57, 58, 59, 60, 61, 62, 72, 73, 127
4.NF.2. Compare two fractions with different numerators and different denominators, e.g., by creating common denominators or numerators, or by comparing to a benchmark fraction such as 1/2. Recognize that comparisons are valid only when the two fractions refer to the same whole. Record the results of comparisons with symbols >, =, or <, and justify the conclusions, e.g., by using a visual fraction model.	51, 56, 57, 58, 59, 60, 61, 62, 73, 127

Build fractions from unit fractions.	
4.NF.3. Understand a fraction *a/b* with *a* > 1 as a sum of fractions 1/*b*.	60, 61, 127
4.NF.4. Apply and extend previous understandings of multiplication to multiply a fraction by a whole number.	122
Understand decimal notation for fractions, and compare decimal fractions.	
4.NF.5. Express a fraction with denominator 10 as an equivalent fraction with denominator 100, and use this technique to add two fractions with respective denominators 10 and 100. *For example, express 3/10 as 30/100, and add 3/10 + 4/100 = 34/100.*	61, 62, 63, 64, 66, 67, 72, 73, 128
4.NF.6. Use decimal notation for fractions with denominators 10 or 100. *For example, rewrite 0.62 as 62/100; describe a length as 0.62 meters; locate 0.62 on a number line diagram.*	61, 62, 63, 64, 66, 67, 72, 73, 74, 128
4.NF.7. Compare two decimals to hundredths by reasoning about their size. Recognize that comparisons are valid only when the two decimals refer to the same whole. Record the results of comparisons with the symbols >, =, or <, and justify the conclusions, e.g., by using a visual model.	62, 65, 66, 67, 72, 73, 74, 128
Measurement & Data	
Solve problems involving measurement and conversion of measurements.	
4.MD.1. Know relative sizes of measurement units within one system of units including km, m, cm; kg, g; lb, oz.; l, ml; hr, min, sec. Within a single system of measurement, express measurements in a larger unit in terms of a smaller unit. Record measurement equivalents in a two-column table. *For example, know that 1 ft is 12 times as long as 1 in. Express the length of a 4 ft snake as 48 in. Generate a conversion table for feet and inches listing the number pairs (1, 12), (2, 24), (3, 36), …*	108, 109
4.MD.2. Use the four operations to solve word problems involving distances, intervals of time, liquid volumes, masses of objects, and money, including problems involving simple fractions or decimals, and problems that require expressing measurements given in a larger unit in terms of a smaller unit. Represent measurement quantities using diagrams such as number line diagrams that feature a measurement scale.	75, 76, 77, 78, 104, 105, 106, 107, 113, 122, 123, 128
4.MD.3. Apply the area and perimeter formulas for rectangles in real world and mathematical problems. *For example, find the width of a rectangular room given the area of the flooring and the length, by viewing the area formula as a multiplication equation with an unknown factor.*	110, 111, 112
Represent and interpret data.	
4.MD.4. Make a line plot to display a data set of measurements in fractions of a unit (1/2, 1/4, 1/8). Solve problems involving addition and subtraction of fractions by using information presented in line plots. *For example, from a line plot find and interpret the difference in length between the longest and shortest specimens in an insect collection.*	116, 117, 118, 119, 120, 121, 122
Geometric measurement: understand concepts of angle and measure angles.	
4.MD.5. Recognize angles as geometric shapes that are formed wherever two rays share a common endpoint, and understand concepts of angle measurement.	83, 84, 85, 86
4.MD.7. Recognize angle measure as additive. When an angle is decomposed into non-overlapping parts, the angle measure of the whole is the sum of the angle measures of the parts. Solve addition and subtraction problems to find unknown angles on a diagram in real world and mathematical problems, e.g., by using an equation with a symbol for the unknown angle measure.	84, 85, 86
Geometry	
Draw and identify lines and angles, and classify shapes by properties of their lines and angles.	
4.G.1. Draw points, lines, line segments, rays, angles (right, acute, obtuse), and perpendicular and parallel lines. Identify these in two-dimensional figures.	80, 81, 82, 83, 84, 85, 86, 87, 90, 91
4.G.2. Classify two-dimensional figures based on the presence or absence of parallel or perpendicular lines, or the presence or absence of angles of a specified size. Recognize right triangles as a category, and identify right triangles.	80, 81, 82, 85, 86, 90, 91
4.G.3. Recognize a line of symmetry for a two-dimensional figure as a line across the figure such that the figure can be folded along the line into matching parts. Identify line-symmetric figures and draw lines of symmetry.	79, 103

Numbers to 9,999

① Write the number shown on each abacus.

a.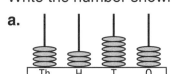

b.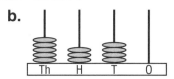

c.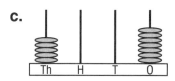

_____   _____   _____

② Draw each number on the abacus.

a. 4,265 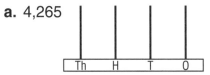   **b.** 1,460    **c.** 2,055

③ Write the numeral for each of the following.

a. seven thousand, three hundred seventy-two _____

b. five thousand, eleven _____

c. two thousand, one hundred one _____

d. two thousand, twenty-one _____

④ Write each of the following numbers in words.

a. 1,275 _____

b. 2,041 _____

c. 7,009 _____

⑤ Draw a line to match each numeral and its name.

a. 4,003   four thousand, thirty

b. 4,013   four thousand, thirty-three

c. 4,030   four thousand, three

d. 4,310   four thousand, three hundred

e. 4,033   four thousand, thirteen

f. 4,300   four thousand, three hundred ten

⑥ Use the digits 6, 7, 3, and 2 to write five 4-digit numbers less than 5,000.

_____; _____; _____; _____; _____

Place Value 0 – 9,999

1 Write the following numbers in the place value chart.

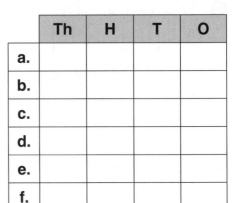

	Th	H	T	O
a.				
b.				
c.				
d.				
e.				
f.				

a. five thousand, ten

b. two thousand, three hundred sixty-one

c. six thousand, two hundred

d. nine thousand, twenty-six

e. three thousand, one hundred eleven

f. four thousand, fifty-seven

2 Complete the numeral expanders for each of the following numbers.

a. 1,239

Th	H	T	O
	H	T	O
		T	O

b. 4,625

Th	H	T	O
	H	T	O
		T	O

c. 8,290

Th	H	T	O
	H	T	O
		T	O

3 Write the value of the underlined digit in each of the following numbers.

a. 2,3<u>6</u>1 _____

b. 4,6<u>9</u>5 _____

c. 6,42<u>5</u> _____

d. <u>8</u>,865 _____

4 Answer *true* or *false* for each of the following.

a. 2,369 > 2,269 _____

b. 1,432 < 1,431 _____

c. 5,768 > 5,786 _____

d. 6,195 > 6,159 _____

e. 6,084 < 6,048 _____

f. 9,020 < 1,920 _____

5 For each set of digits, make the smallest possible 4-digit number.

a. 4, 8, 7, 3 _____

b. 9, 0, 9, 6 _____

c. 4, 5, 6, 1 _____

d. 6, 2, 4, 8 _____

6 Write a.–e. as numerals and then arrange the numbers from least to greatest (f.).

a. four thousand, seventy-two _____

b. four thousand, one hundred twelve _____

c. four thousand, nineteen _____

d. four thousand, ninety _____

e. four thousand, two hundred _____

f. Least to greatest: _____

Ordering Numbers

❶ Complete the following number patterns.

a.

8,002	8,004	8,006		

b.

4,010	4,015	4,020		

c.

6,090	6,089	6,088		

d.

3,100	3,090	3,080		

❷ Order each group of numbers from least to greatest.

a. 2,045; 2,010; 2,100; 2,076 _____

b. 1,147; 1,129; 1,176; 1,010 _____

c. 4,206; 2,046; 6,402; 6,024 _____

d. 9,342; 9,432; 9,234; 9,324 _____

e. 6,066; 6,606; 6,660; 6,006 _____

f. 2,469; 3,841; 8,691; 1,428 _____

❸ Write the missing numbers in the spaces.

a.

1,241	1,341		1,541	

b.

2,028	2,038		2,058	

c.

1,006		3,006	4,006	

d.

9,416		9,436	9,446	

❹ Order each group of numbers from greatest to least.

a. 2,220; 2,210; 2,232; 2,206 _____

b. 7,860; 6,870; 6,780; 8,760 _____

c. 4,503; 4,609; 4,805; 4,302 _____

d. 1,111; 1,101; 1,011; 1,010 _____

e. 6,326; 5,245; 8,691; 7,589 _____

f. 1,980; 1,976; 1,998; 1,989 _____

❺ Joel had a stack of *Fun Times* magazines that he wanted to place in order on his bookshelf. Each magazine was from a different year. Order the magazines from oldest to newest.

2009	1999	2010

2006	2012	1998

_____

❻ Start at 1,359 and count forward by tens. Write the next five numbers in the pattern.

1,359; _____; _____; _____; _____; _____

Counting by Thousands

1 Round each of the following numbers to the nearest thousand.

    a. 4,072 _____
    b. 6,985 _____
    c. 3,821 _____

    d. 8,180 _____
    e. 2,222 _____
    f. 7,925 _____

2 Write the number that is 1,000 more than:

    a. 6,210 _____
    b. 8,672 _____
    c. 1,029 _____

    d. 4,276 _____
    e. 5,006 _____
    f. 2,407 _____

3 Write the number that is 1,000 less than:

    a. 4,675 _____
    b. 3,346 _____
    c. 9,832 _____

    d. 2,401 _____
    e. 5,050 _____
    f. 6,011 _____

4 Complete the following patterns.

a.

1,265	2,265	3,265		

b.

5,050	6,050	7,050		

c.

3,111	4,111	5,111		

d.

9,532	8,532	7,532		

e.

5,781	4,781	3,781		

f.

7,006	6,006	5,006		

5 In words, write the number that is one thousand more than the following.

    a. six thousand, two hundred seventy-two _____

    _____

    b. nine hundred fifty-three _____

    _____

6 In words, write the number that is one thousand less than the following.

    a. three thousand, four hundred five _____

    _____

    b. four thousand, nineteen _____

    _____

Expanding 4-Digit Numbers

❶ Use the numeral expander to expand the following numbers.

a. 1,426 | Th | H | T | 0 | **b.** 6,349 | Th | H | T | 0 |

c. 8,273 | Th | H | T | 0 | **d.** 4,201 | Th | H | T | 0 |

❷ Write the numeral for the following.

a. 1,000 + 300 + 60 + 5 _____ **b.** 4,000 + 900 + 70 + 6 _____

c. 7,000 + 500 + 30 + 1 _____ **d.** 5,000 + 60 + 7 _____

e. 7,000 + 400 + 60 _____ **f.** 800 + 70 + 2 _____

❸ Write the place value of each underlined digit.

a. 3,2<u>5</u>1 _____ **b.** 4,<u>1</u>06 _____

c. 2,98<u>7</u> _____ **d.** <u>8</u>,499 _____

❹ Write the following numbers in expanded form.

a. 1,296 _____

b. 5,257 _____

c. 9,021 _____

d. 2,999 _____

e. 8,501 _____

f. 6,790 _____

❺ Write the following numbers in expanded form.

a. two thousand, five hundred twenty-one _____

b. five thousand, seventy-eight _____

c. seven thousand, one hundred one _____

d. nine thousand, three hundred _____

❻ Represent 7,000 + 400 + 6 on the abacus.

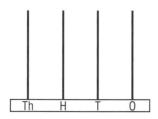

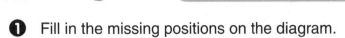

Ordinal Numbers

❶ Fill in the missing positions on the diagram.

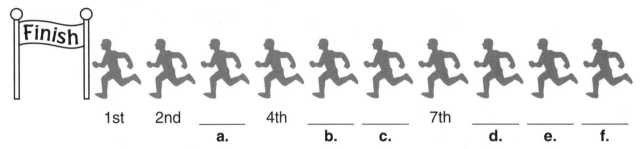

1st   2nd   _____   4th   _____   _____   7th   _____   _____   _____
              a.   **b.**   **c.**   **d.**   **e.**   **f.**

❷ If 8 people ran in a sprint race,

  a. what position is the winner? _____

  b. what is the last position? _____

  c. what position is after 5th? _____

  d. what position is before 8th? _____

❸ If 100 people ran in a marathon,

  a. what position is the winner? _____

  b. what is the last position? _____

  c. what position is after 11th? _____

  d. what position is after 20th? _____

  e. what are the positions of the last five runners?

  f. what positions are between 11th and 17th?

  _____   _____

❹ Write the following as ordinal numbers.

  a. third _____   **b.** fifth _____   **c.** first _____

  d. eleventh _____   **e.** twentieth _____   **f.** fiftieth _____

❺ Write the ordinal numbers (in order) to represent the positions of 20 people standing in line.

  _____

  _____

❻ There are five pigs in a race. Draw the pigs and write the positions of the first three across the finish line.

Doubling and Halving

❶ Use doubles (multiplying by 2) to complete the following. The first one has been started for you.

a.   4 × 10

double 10 = ___20___

double ___20___ = _____

4 × 10 = _____

b.   4 × 15

double 15 = _____

double _____ = _____

4 × 15 = _____

c.   4 × 21

double 21 = _____

double _____ = _____

4 × 21 = _____

d.   4 × 30

double 30 = _____

double _____ = _____

4 × 30 = _____

❷ Find how many total legs on the following groups of animals. Use the doubling method, if needed.

a. How many legs on 16 goats? _____

b. How many legs on 25 dogs? _____

c. How many legs on 50 cats? _____

d. How many legs on 40 tigers? _____

❸ What number is halfway between the following numbers?

a. 0 and 50 _____

b. 50 and 100 _____

c. 1,000 and 5,000 _____

d. 7,000 and 8,000 _____

e. 900 and 1,000 _____

f. 400 and 600 _____

❹ What is half of the following?

a. 16 apples _____

b. 300 bananas _____

c. 500 grapes _____

d. 50 oranges _____

❺ Use doubles to find the following.

a. 8 × 25 _____

b. 16 × 21 _____

❻ Find half of the following to find one person's share.

a. 2 people sharing 40 books _____

b. 2 people sharing 70 marbles _____

Less Than and Greater Than

1 Write the number that is 5 greater than:

    a. 110 _____   **b.** 997 _____

    c. 1,015 _____   **d.** 2,851 _____

    e. 3,694 _____   **f.** 2,328 _____

2 Write the number that is 5 less than:

    a. 601 _____   **b.** 993 _____

    c. 1,004 _____   **d.** 2,855 _____

    e. 3,762 _____   **f.** 2,111 _____

3 True or false?

    a. 863 < 683 _____   **b.** 2,140 < 2,130 _____

    c. 999 < 990 _____   **d.** 1,101 > 1,110 _____

    e. 3,469 < 3,496 _____   **f.** 2,751 > 2,571 _____

4 Use the correct sign, < or >, to make the following number statements true.

    a. 410 ☐ 411   **b.** 856 ☐ 865

    c. 1,250 ☐ 1,240   **d.** 1,349 ☐ 1,439

    e. 9,256 ☐ 9,236   **f.** 3,751 ☐ 3,715

5 Write a number in the box to make each number statement true.

    a. 2,499 > ☐   **b.** ☐ < 3,677

    c. 4,271 < ☐   **d.** ☐ > 6,279

6 Write the following numbers in standard form, and then write two correct < or > statements using the digits.

    a. one thousand, four hundred eleven _____

    b. one thousand, eight hundred nine _____

    c. two thousand, six hundred fifty _____

    d. _____   _____

Number Patterns

❶ Complete each number pattern.

a.
14	18	22		

b.
110	105	100		

c.
24	34	44		

d.
124	224	324		

e.
1,426	2,426	3,426		

f.
5,526	4,526	3,526		

❷ Write the first five terms in each of the following number patterns.

a. start at 100 and count by threes _____, _____, _____, _____, _____

b. start at 17 and count by fours _____, _____, _____, _____, _____

c. start at 100 and count backwards by fives _____, _____, _____, _____, _____

d. start at 80 and count backwards by twos _____, _____, _____, _____, _____

e. start at 3,416 and count by hundreds _____; _____; _____; _____; _____

f. start at 256 and count backwards by tens _____, _____, _____, _____, _____

❸ Find the rule for each of the number patterns.

a. 150, 200, 250, 300 _____

b. 500, 520, 540, 560 _____

c. 77, 70, 63, 56 _____

d. 999, 990, 981, 972 _____

e. 1,365; 1,265; 1,165; 1,065 _____

f. 2,125; 2,135; 2,145; 2,155 _____

❹ Fill in the missing numbers in each pattern.

a.
20		60		100

b.
597	589			565

c.
24	32		48	

d.
$1\frac{1}{2}$	$2\frac{1}{2}$			$5\frac{1}{2}$

e.
$\frac{1}{2}$	1		2	

f.
1,560		1,572		1,584

❺ Write the tenth term in each number pattern.

a. 9, 18, 27, 36, . . . _____

b. 8, 16, 24, 32, . . . _____

c. 10, 20, 30, 40, . . . _____

d. 15, 25, 35, 45, . . . _____

❻ Starting at 100, count backwards by nines and find the tenth term.

100, _____, _____, _____, _____, _____, _____, _____, _____, _____

1 Complete each of the following.

   a.   4 tens and 3 ones
       + 3 tens and 6 ones

   b.   6 tens and 4 ones
       + 1 ten and 3 ones

   c.   3 tens and 5 ones
       + 2 tens and 1 one

2 Add the following.

a.	**b.**	**c.**	**d.**	**e.**	**f.**
41	23	15	13	65	44
+ 36	+ 71	+ 20	+ 81	+ 30	+ 44

3 Add the following.

a. 61 + 31 = _____

b. 28 + 41 = _____

c. 90 + 9 = _____

d. 70 + 18 = _____

e. 73 + 15 = _____

f. 62 + 35 = _____

4 Solve each of the following.

  a. Veronica had 32 stickers, and Yuko had 25. How many stickers were there altogether? _____

  b. There were 42 cows on one farm and 38 on another. How many cows were there in all? _____

  c. In a fruit box, there were 18 oranges and 25 apples. How many total fruits were there? _____

5 (15) (23) (37) (46) (29) (53)

From the numbers above, find two numbers that total:

a. 68 = _____

b. 60 = _____

c. 69 = _____

d. 75 = _____

6 Find the missing number in each equation.

a. 24 = 13 + ☐

b. 47 + ☐ = 59

c. 15 + ☐ = 53

d. ☐ + 14 = 82

Adding to 999

❶ Estimate the sums by first rounding all numbers to the nearest ten. Then find the exact sums.

		Estimate	Answer
a.	55 + 21 + 11		
b.	61 + 25 + 10		
c.	12 + 17 + 50		
d.	19 + 20 + 40		

❷ Add the following.

a. 426
  + 371

b. 614
  + 323

c. 727
  + 272

d. 114
  + 863

e. 785
  + 210

f. 306
  + 290

❸ Add the following.

a. 120 + 50 = _____

b. 675 + 30 = _____

c. 215 + 80 = _____

d. 195 + 203 = _____

❹ Find the missing numbers to make each problem correct.

a. 658
  + _3_
   7_8

b. 722
  + 2_5
   _6_

c. 4_3
  + 29_
   _97

d. 17_
  + 2_5
   _88

❺ Find the sums of the following doubles.

a. 321
  + 321

b. 243
  + 243

c. 413
  + 413

d. 104
  + 104

❻ Munir had 214 cards in his collection. One year later, he had doubled his collection. How many cards did he have altogether?

_____

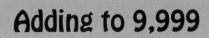

❶ Add the following.

a. 5,260 + 2,000 = _____   **b.** 7,849 + 1,000 = _____

c. 2,692 + 7,000 = _____   **d.** 5,360 + 300 = _____

e. 7,450 + 500 = _____   **f.** 3,650 + 200 = _____

❷ Add the following.

a. 1,673
  +3,026

b. 3,491
  +2,305

c. 7,528
  +1,360

d. 4,687
  +3,212

e. 5,325
  +1,321

f. 4,976
  +4,021

❸ Complete each of the following.

a. Add 4,236 and 1,350. _____

b. Find the sum of 2,153 and 6,325. _____

c. Find the total of 8,543 and 1,352. _____

d. Find 3,468 plus 1,221. _____

❹ What must be added to the following to make 999?

a. 630 _____   **b.** 246 _____

c. 928 _____   **d.** 755 _____

❺ In one box, there were 2,467 paper clips. In a
second box, there were 2,321 paper clips. How
many paper clips were there altogether?   _____

❻ What is the total of the following numbers?

• one thousand, three hundred twenty-five

• two thousand, four hundred eleven

• three thousand, one hundred thirty-two   Total = _____

Adding with Regrouping to 999

1 Add the following.

  a.   615
      +225

  b.   752
      +109

  c.   193
      +151

  d.   376
      +430

  e.   587
      +244

  f.   198
      +223

2 Add the following.

  a. 428 + 108 = _____

  b. 473 + 429 = _____

  c. 172 + 356 = _____

  d. 725 + 192 = _____

  e. 166 + 255 = _____

  f. 159 + 793 = _____

3 Complete the following.

a.

+	129	246	326	418
65				

b.

+	91	372	585	755
164				

4 Complete each of the following.

  a. Add 152 and 109. _____

  b. Find the sum of 226 and 438. _____

  c. What is 256 plus 375? _____

  d. Find the total of 743 and 157. _____

5 Find the total number of items.

  a. 245 nails and 269 tacks _____

  b. 129 pens and 457 pencils _____

  c. 385 cookies and 45 cakes _____

  d. 690 mice and 156 rats _____

6 The school has boxes of toys. Counted together, which of the following items give a:

295 dice	86 tops	173 pencils

  a. total of 468? _____

  b. total of 259? _____

  c. total of 554? _____

Adding Three Numbers

1 Add the following.

a. 2,062	b. 3,250	c. 1,905	d. 3,333
1,524	1,905	2,063	2,136
+1,460	+2,153	+4,012	+4,325

2 How many were there altogether if:

a. on Monday 1,236 newspapers were delivered; Wednesday 2,315; and Friday 1,321? _____

b. in the pet shop there were 496 fish in one tank, 327 in another, and 537 in a third? _____

c. the number of lemons picked on three different days were 1,379; 2,450; and 1,856? _____

d. in three different piles of paper, there were 2,136; 3,215; and 1,469 sheets of paper? _____

3 Using addition, find the total of 3 groups of:

a. 1,210 _____   **b.** 2,401 _____

c. 3,010 _____   **d.** 1,234 _____

4 Find the sum. Then find what must be added to the sum to make 9,999.

a. 3,050 + 2,690 = _____ + _____ = 9,999

b. 5,631 + 2,506 = _____ + _____ = 9,999

c. 3,625 + 1,375 = _____ + _____ = 9,999

d. 1,982 + 5,385 = _____ + _____ = 9,999

5 Calculate the total cost of the following purchase.

game console	$299
stereo	$185
flat-screen TV	$1,346

_____

6 Write an addition word problem using the numbers 1,372; 4,685; and 3,201. Then solve it.

_____

_____

_____

❶ Add the following.

a.	3,864	b.	1,452	c.	3,847	d.	1,385
	1,972		1,799		2,418		1,268
	+1,085		+5,006		+1,385		+1,101

❷ Complete each of the following.

a. Add 3,245; 1,609; and 1,210. _____

b. Find the sum of 2,468; 1,357; and 1,204. _____

c. Find the total of 2,731; 1,046; and 1,205. _____

d. Find 998 plus 3,256 plus 1,467. _____

❸ Find the total cost.

a. $1,321; $4,653; and $3,201 _____   b. $1,111; $2,010; and $3,501 _____

c. $999; $2,995; and $2,050 _____   d. $5,995; $1,010; and $995 _____

❹ Add the following.

a.	123	b.	456	c.	752
	436		298		171
	129		105		333
	+ 46		+150		+205

d.	1,025	e.	2,905	f.	2,050
	985		350		1,060
	103		725		4,250
	+ 856		+ 430		+ 990

❺ In one hour, we counted 250 cars, 103 trucks, 23 motorcycles, 6 emergency vehicles, and 5 buses as they drove by the school. What was the total number of vehicles for that hour? _____

❻ Write an addition word problem using the numbers 3,250; 1,075; 495; and 2,860. Then solve it.

_____

_____

Rounding Numbers

1   **a.** Is 498 closer to 400 or 500? _____

      b. Is 732 closer to 700 or 800? _____

      c. Is 221 closer to 200 or 300? _____

      d. Is 1,350 closer to 1,000 or 2,000? _____

      e. Is 2,830 closer to 2,000 or 3,000? _____

      f. Is 7,795 closer to 7,000 or 8,000? _____

2   Which of the following numbers round to 4,000? Circle them.

      a. 3,956   **b.** 3,275   **c.** 4,835

      d. 4,163   **e.** 3,709   **f.** 4,550

3   Each of the following numbers are rounded to the nearest thousand. Answer *true* or *false*.

      a. 3,259 rounds to 3,000 _____   **b.** 4,635 rounds to 4,000 _____

      c. 7,856 rounds to 8,000 _____   **d.** 9,015 rounds to 9,000 _____

4   Round each number to the nearest ten.

      a. 67 _____   **b.** 153 _____   **c.** 278 _____

      d. 5,133 _____   **e.** 7,596 _____   **f.** 2,992 _____

5   Round each number to the nearest hundred.

      a. 127 _____   **b.** 572 _____   **c.** 885 _____

      d. 5,610 _____   **e.** 8,374 _____   **f.** 6,019 _____

6   **a.** Round each number to the nearest hundred: 1,496; 2,019; 3,725; 915

      _____

      b. Add the rounded numbers together. _____

      c. If this total was subtracted from 9,000, how much would be left? _____

Subtracting 2-Digit Numbers without Regrouping

❶ Subtract the following.

a. 58 – 23 = _____

b. 69 – 24 = _____

c. 49 – 16 = _____

d. 87 – 55 = _____

e. 67 – 43 = _____

f. 75 – 31 = _____

❷ Complete the following.

a.

–	56	73	85	49
21				

b.

–	46	29	34	78
13				

❸ Subtract the following.

a. 56
      – 2 3

b. 7 3
      – 4 1

c. 5 7
      – 4 3

d. 6 9
      – 4 3

e. 8 9
      – 3 5

f. 9 8
      – 4 2

❹ How many were left if:

a. Sandy had 66 sheep and she sold 34? _____

b. there were 24 chocolates in the box and 13 were eaten? _____

c. from a pack of 52 cards, 11 were lost? _____

d. on a flower stand, there were 58 bunches of flowers and 37 bunches were sold? _____

❺ Brandon bought lunch for him and his friends for a total of $19. If he paid with a $50 bill, how much change did he get back? _____

❻ If I take 43 from a number, then double the answer, I get 26. What is the number? _____

Subtracting with Regrouping

❶ Subtract the following.

a.   4 6
   – 2 7
	b. 5 7
	   – 3 9
		c. 8 1
		   – 4 4

d.   7 2
   – 3 8
	e. 8 6
	   – 6 9
		f. 8 2
		   – 2 4

❷ Subtract the following.

a. $46 - 29 =$ _____

b. $36 - 18 =$ _____

c. $72 - 54 =$ _____

d. $65 - 38 =$ _____

❸ Some children are saving for scooters that cost $92. How much more does each child need to save if:

a. Arthur has $45? _____

b. Payal has $38? _____

c. Thomas has $18? _____

d. Lily has $79? _____

❹ Find the missing numbers.

a.   7 7
   – ☐
   3 4
	b. 9 5
	   – ☐
	   7 0
		c. 6 3
		   – ☐
		   1 2
			d. 8 7
			   – ☐
			   3 1

❺ True or false?

a. $81 - 37 < 52 - 25$ _____

b. $86 - 49 > 85 - 47$ _____

c. $77 - 39 > 99 - 62$ _____

❻ Two 3-digit numbers have a difference of 132. The first number has 6 in the ones place. The second number has a 2 in the hundreds place and a 3 in the tens place. What is the equation with the missing numbers?

_____

1 Subtract the following.

a.
```
   856
 –  43
```

b.
```
   927
 –  16
```

c.
```
   698
 –  67
```

d.
```
   778
 – 604
```

e.
```
   369
 – 127
```

f.
```
   273
 – 150
```

2 Find the following.

a. 945 minus 32 _____

b. 165 take away 45 _____

c. subtract 52 from 173 _____

d. the difference between 276 and 51 _____

e. 18 less than 499 _____

f. How much greater is 189 than 56? _____

3 Subtract the following amounts.

a. $256 – $123 _____

b. $379 – $146 _____

c. $852 – $711 _____

d. $799 – $185 _____

4 Find the missing numbers.

a.
```
   156
 – _3
  11_
```

b.
```
   689
 – _2
  60_
```

c.
```
   39_
 – _7
  332
```

d.
```
   195
 – 7_
  1_1
```

e.
```
   732
 – _2
  71_
```

f.
```
   529
 – __
  500
```

5 Solve the following.

a. A brick wall had 569 bricks, but 352 were knocked off. How many were left? _____

b. A floor had 525 tiles, but 214 were replaced with wood. How many tiles were left? _____

c. A school had 649 students. 336 were girls. How many were boys? _____

d. Simone has 713 stamps. How many more does she need to have 966? _____

6 Write a list of words or phrases that mean *subtract*.

_____

_____

Subtracting 3-Digit Numbers with Regrouping

1 Subtract the following.

a. 545
−219

b. 684
−278

c. 215
−170

d. 729
−238

e. 715
−477

f. 624
−435

2 Find the following.

a. 733 minus 242 _____

b. 916 take away 836 _____

c. 605 subtract 413 _____

d. the difference between 401 and 153 _____

e. 214 less 175 _____

f. subtract 498 from 600 _____

3 At the State Fair, there were 852 cows, 735 sheep, 127 pigs, and 463 goats. How many more:

a. cows than sheep? _____

b. sheep than pigs? _____

c. sheep than goats? _____

d. cows than goats? _____

4 Check the following subtraction equations with addition.

a. 142
− 61 | + 61

b. 245
− 163 | + 163

c. 475
− 229 | + 229

d. 381
− 118 | + 118

e. 901
− 182 | + 182

f. 800
− 321 | + 321

5 If I started with $350, find how much I would have left if I spent:

a. $270? _____

b. $125? _____

c. $295? _____

d. $317? _____

6 Find the difference between: two hundred seventy-five and one hundred sixty-eight. Write your answer in words.

_____

Subtracting without Regrouping to 9,999

1 Subtract the following.

a.	3,8 3 4	b.	3,9 4 5	c.	6,3 5 8
	− 2,3 1 2		− 2,8 1 0		− 5,1 2 6

d.	9,9 9 9	e.	6,7 5 0	f.	3,9 2 9
	− 7,6 5 3		− 4,5 1 0		− 1,4 1 7

2 Subtract the following.

a. 6,351 − 4,210 = _____   **b.** 7,985 − 6,324 = _____

c. 6,385 − 5,184 = _____   **d.** 9,469 − 7,325 = _____

3 Find the missing numbers.

a.	4,6 2 7	b.	7,4 9 3	c.	8,3 5 6
	− 2,_ 1 _		− 6,_ 4 _		− _,1 _ 4
	_,3 _ 1		_,2 _ 0		7,_ 1 _

d.	9,8 5 2	e.	5,_ 7 _	f.	_,9 _ 4
	− _,6 _ 1		− 2,4 1 5		− 4,_ 0 2
	3,_ 1 _		_,3 _ 1		4,6 1 _

4 Estimate to the nearest thousand, and then calculate the exact answer.

a. Tilly has $4,920. How much more does she need to have $9,951?

_____, _____

b. Caitlin has 3,456 marbles. Erin has 2,315. How many more marbles does Caitlin have? _____, _____

c. The warehouse has 4,956 cans of beans. If it has a total of 8,977 cans, how many are not beans? _____, _____

5 Using the digits 4, 6, 3, and 1, write:

a. the largest 4-digit number. _____

b. the smallest 4-digit number. _____

c. Find the difference between the two numbers. _____

6 Make up a subtraction word problem using the numbers 7,959 and 3,416. Then solve it.

_____

_____

1 Subtract the following.

a. 4,365
   − 1,285
   _____

b. 5,472
   − 4,319
   _____

c. 6,719
   − 3,273
   _____

d. 3,000
   − 1,451
   _____

e. 2,637
   − 1,908
   _____

f. 8,754
   − 5,276
   _____

2 Find the following.

a. 6,050 minus 2,351. _____

b. 7,125 take away 2,346. _____

c. 8,943 subtract 3,785. _____

d. The difference between 4,637 and 1,952. _____

e. Subtract 4,259 from 6,463. _____

f. 9,221 less 4,635. _____

3 Find the difference between 5,000 and:

a. 2,451. _____

b. 1,985. _____

c. 4,201. _____

d. 3,625. _____

4 Subtract the following amounts.

a. $3,250 − $1,985 = _____

b. $9,900 − $6,095 = _____

c. $4,250 − $1,475 = _____

d. $5,895 − $3,956 = _____

5 **a.** Find the total cost of the below items. _____

camera
$299

scanner
$975

printer
$1,250

b. If I had $7,000, how much would I have after buying all of the above items? _____

6 Find the difference between: three thousand, one hundred seven and one thousand, two hundred fifty-nine. Write your answer in words.

_____

_____

Rounding Numbers and Estimating

① Round each number to the nearest ten.

a. 1,289 _____   **b.** 1,756 _____   **c.** 2,372 _____

d. 4,921 _____   **e.** 6,208 _____   **f.** 5,201 _____

② Round numbers to the nearest ten and circle the best estimate for the sum.

a. 9 + 15 + 200 + 48 _____	260	280	300
b. 49 + 98 + 201 _____	350	370	390
c. 121 + 57 + 309 _____	450	470	490
d. 132 + 132 + 132 + 132 _____	480	500	520
e. 197 + 197 + 197 + 197 _____	770	800	830
f. 73 + 73 + 73 + 73 _____	280	300	320

③ Round numbers to the nearest ten and circle the best estimate for the difference.

a. 100 − 9 − 9 − 9 − 9 − 9 − 9 _____	30	40	50
b. 200 − 31 − 31 − 31 − 31 _____	60	80	100
c. 500 − 57 − 57 − 57 − 57 _____	260	270	280
d. 100 − 34 − 14 − 9 _____	40	50	60
e. 200 − 59 − 24 − 11 _____	90	110	130
f. 500 − 182 − 59 − 62 _____	180	200	220

④ Round each number to the nearest ten and then estimate the answer.

a. 27 + 51 = _____   **b.** 412 + 93 = _____

c. 238 + 149 = _____   **d.** 298 − 61 = _____

e. 144 − 38 = _____   **f.** 517 − 106 = _____

⑤ Complete the following table, estimating numbers to the nearest ten before calculating actual answers and finding the differences between the two.

	Question	Estimate	Actual	Difference
a.	129 + 32			
b.	319 + 56			
c.	253 − 139			
d.	578 − 304			

⑥ Round each number to the nearest hundred and then estimate the sum. Check the actual answers with a calculator.

a. 578 + 203 + 1,432 + 1,098 = _____, _____

b. 2,751 + 499 + 349 + 1,257 = _____, _____

c. 708 + 211 + 3,560 + 2,188 = _____, _____

Multiplication with Modeling and Mental Strategies

❶ Complete the following number sentences to find the total number of dots.

a.

3 groups of 4 dots = _____

b.

6 groups of 2 dots = _____

c.

4 groups of ____ dots = ____

d.

3 groups of ___ dots = ___

e.

___ groups of ___ dots = ___

f.

___ groups of ___ dot = ___

❷ Write a number sentence for each array.

a.

b.

c.

d.

_____   _____   _____   _____

❸ Large multiplication equations can be split into tens and ones components, each calculated and added together. Complete the following using this strategy.

a. 14×8
$= (10 \times 8) + (4 \times 8)$
$=$ _____ + _____
$=$ _____

b. 15×9
$= (10 \times 9) + (5 \times 9)$
$=$ _____ + _____
$=$ _____

c. 13×6
$= (10 \times 6) + (3 \times 6)$
$=$ _____ + _____
$=$ _____

d. 16×7
$= (10 \times 7) + (6 \times 7)$
$=$ _____ + _____
$=$ _____

e. 18×5
$= (10 \times 5) + (8 \times 5)$
$=$ _____ + _____
$=$ _____

f. 17×8
$= (10 \times 8) + (7 \times 8)$
$=$ _____ + _____
$=$ _____

❹ Use doubles to calculate the following. The first one has been started for you.

a. double 21 = ____42____
double ____42____ = _____
$4 \times 21 =$ _____

b. double 16 = _____
double _____ = _____
$4 \times 16 =$ _____

c. double 15 = _____
double _____ = _____
$4 \times 15 =$ _____

d. double 33 = _____
double _____ = _____
$4 \times 33 =$ _____

❺ Using triangles, draw the following.

a. 4 groups of 5

b. 3×6 array

❻ Use doubles to find the following.

a. 8×22 _____

b. 8×31 _____

1 Divide each number in half and repeat for as long as the numbers are whole (i.e., no fractions or decimals).

    a. 16 _____

    b. 100 _____

    c. 160 _____

    d. 256 _____

2 Double the number and keep doubling five times for each number.

    a. 9 _____

    b. 4 _____

    c. 5 _____

    d. 100 _____

3 Are the following number sentences true or false?

    a. $222 - 22 = 200$ _____   **b.** $2 \times 22 = 22 + 22$ _____

    c. $22 \div 2 = 2 \div 22$ _____   **d.** $222 - 2 = 22$ _____

    e. $22 + 22 + 22 = 3 \times 22$ _____   **f.** $22 - 2 = 2 - 22$ _____

4 Are the following number sentences true or false?

    a. $14 + 21 = 21 + 14$ _____   **b.** $14 \times 21 = 21 \times 14$ _____

    c. $21 - 14 = 14 - 21$ _____   **d.** $21 \div 7 = 7 \div 21$ _____

    e. $7 + 7 + 7 = 3 \times 7$ _____   **f.** $121 - 14 = 14 - 121$ _____

5 Find the mistake in the equation, and correct it.

$$\begin{array}{r} 459 \\ +\,107 \\ \hline 666 \end{array}$$

6 Find the mistake in the equation, and correct it.

$$\begin{array}{r} 374 \\ -\,135 \\ \hline 249 \end{array}$$

❶ Find the product of the following numbers.

a. 5 and 4 _____

b. 10 and 8 _____

c. 3 and 2 _____

d. 12 and 4 _____

e. 10 and 2 _____

f. 7 and 8 _____

❷ Multiply the following.

a. $3 \times 8 =$ _____

b. $6 \times 2 =$ _____

c. $9 \times 4 =$ _____

d. $11 \times 2 =$ _____

e. $3 \times 4 =$ _____

f. $5 \times 8 =$ _____

❸ Find the number of legs on:

a. 9 spiders _____

b. 12 chickens _____

c. 6 sheep _____

d. 1 flamingo _____

e. 8 cows _____

f. 4 insects _____

❹ Write the first 10 multiples of the following numbers.

a. 1 _____

b. 2 _____

c. 4 _____

d. 8 _____

❺ There were 5 spiders, 3 cats, 4 dogs, and 9 birds on display in a tent at the pet show. How many legs were there altogether? _____

❻ There were 10 cars and 12 bicycles in a small parking lot. How many total wheels were there? _____

Multiplication (× 5 and × 10)

1 Multiply the following.

    a. $3 \times 5 =$ _____   **b.** $10 \times 10 =$ _____

    c. $12 \times 5 =$ _____   **d.** $2 \times 10 =$ _____

    e. $5 \times 0 =$ _____   **f.** $7 \times 10 =$ _____

2 Find:

    a. the product of 11 and 5. _____   **b.** 6 groups of 10. _____

    c. 9 multiplied by 5. _____   **d.** 11 times 10. _____

3 True or false?

    a. $2 \times 5 = 1 \times 10$ _____   **b.** $7 \times 5 = 7 \times 10$ _____

    c. $9 \times 10 = 10 \times 9$ _____   **d.** $8 \times 5 = 4 \times 10$ _____

    e. $6 \times 5 = 5 \times 8$ _____   **f.** $10 \times 5 = 2 \times 10$ _____

4 Complete the following multiplication wheels.

    a.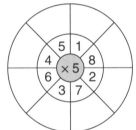   **b.**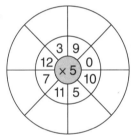

    c.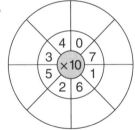   **d.**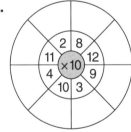

5 Write the first 10 multiples of:

    a. 5: _____

    b. 10: _____

6   **a.** Jan bought 4 bags of oranges from the grocery store. If each bag had 5 oranges, how many oranges did Jan buy in all? _____

    b. Vern bought 10 boxes of granola bars to take on the camping trip. If each box had 6 granola bars, how many total granola bars did Vern buy? _____

Multiplication (× 3, × 6, and × 9)

❶ Multiply the following.

   a. $0 \times 3 =$ _____

   c. $7 \times 9 =$ _____

   e. $6 \times 7 =$ _____

   b. $12 \times 6 =$ _____

   d. $10 \times 3 =$ _____

   f. $9 \times 5 =$ _____

❷ Find the missing numbers.

   a. $3 \times$ _____ $= 12 =$ _____ $\times 6$

   c. $6 \times$ _____ $=$ _____ $= 4 \times 9$

   e. $9 \times$ _____ $= 9 = 3 \times$ _____

   b. $10 \times$ _____ $= 30 =$ _____ $\times 5$

   d. $6 \times 3 =$ _____ $= 9 \times$ _____

   f. $6 \times 4 =$ _____ $= 3 \times$ _____

❸ Find the missing numbers.

   a. $3 \times 9 = 30 -$ _____ $=$ _____

   c. $5 \times 9 = 50 -$ _____ $=$ _____

   e. $6 \times 9 = 60 -$ _____ $=$ _____

   b. $9 \times 9 = 90 -$ _____ $=$ _____

   d. $10 \times 9 = 100 -$ _____ $=$ _____

   f. $11 \times 9 = 110 -$ _____ $=$ _____

❹ Write an equation to show each of the following, and then solve each one.

   a. legs on 9 chickens _____

   b. legs on 8 insects _____

   c. corners on 7 triangles _____

   d. eyes on 6 pandas _____

   e. days in 9 weeks _____

   f. wheels on 11 tricycles _____

❺ **a.** Sara bought 3 movie tickets for $9 each. How much did Sara spend in all? _____

   b. Movie Land was selling old DVDs for $3 each. Dan bought 4 of them. How much did Dan spend on DVDs? _____

   c. At the bake sale, Jenna bought 5 dozen cupcakes for $6 per dozen. How much did Jenna pay for cupcakes? _____

❻ Write three different multiplication equations that have an answer of 28.

_____

1 Multiply the following.

    a. $7 \times 5 =$ _____   **b.** $8 \times 9 =$ _____

    c. $2 \times 8 =$ _____   **d.** $10 \times 7 =$ _____

    e. $6 \times 8 =$ _____   **f.** $3 \times 9 =$ _____

2 True or false?

    a. $7 \times 7 = 8 \times 7$ _____   **b.** $7 \times 4 = 3 \times 8$ _____

    c. $0 \times 9 = 0 \times 7$ _____   **d.** $6 \times 9 = 9 \times 6$ _____

    e. $7 \times 8 = 8 \times 9$ _____   **f.** $4 \times 9 = 9 \times 4$ _____

3 Find the product of the following numbers.

    a. 9 and 7 _____   **b.** 1 and 8 _____

    c. 9 and 5 _____   **d.** 7 and 3 _____

    e. 5 and 8 _____   **f.** 8 and 0 _____

4 Complete the following multiplication wheels.

    a.   **b.**   **c.**

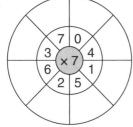 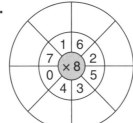 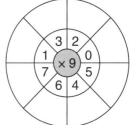

    d.   **e.**   **f.**

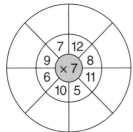 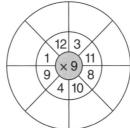 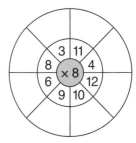

5 Count by eights starting at 50. Write down the next 10 numbers.

    50, _____, _____, _____, _____, _____, _____, _____, _____, _____, _____

6 Count by sevens starting at 30. Write down the next 10 numbers.

    30, _____, _____, _____, _____, _____, _____, _____, _____, _____, _____

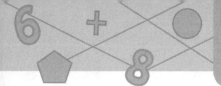

Multiplication

❶ Multiply the following.

a. 6
   × 2
   ___

b. 1 0
   × 8
   ___

c. 9
   × 5
   ___

d. 8
   × 5
   ___

e. 9
   × 7
   ___

f. 3
   × 4
   ___

❷ Complete the multiplication charts.

a.
×	1	2	3	4
2				

b.
×	0	1	2	3
7				

c.
×	6	7	8	9
8				

d.
×	8	9	10	11
5				

e.
×	6	7	8	9
3				

f.
×	5	6	7	8
9				

❸ Find the following totals.

a. 7 groups of 4 _____

b. 8 groups of 6 _____

c. 6 groups of 10 _____

d. 12 groups of 5 _____

e. 4 groups of 8 _____

f. 8 groups of 2 _____

❹ Find the missing numbers.

a. $4 \times 7 =$ _____ $= 7 \times$ _____

b. $10 \times 3 =$ _____ $= 6 \times$ _____

c. $5 \times$ _____ $= 40 = 4 \times$ _____

d. $4 \times$ _____ $= 20 = 2 \times$ _____

e. $9 \times$ _____ $=$ _____ $= 3 \times 6$

f. _____ $\times 4 = 36 = 6 \times$ _____

❺ Find the total cost of the following purchases.

a. 6 movie tickets at $8 each _____

b. 5 caps at $5 each _____

c. 7 chocolate bars at $2 each _____

d. 4 books at $9 each _____

e. 9 T-shirts at $10 each _____

f. 5 sandwiches at $4 each _____

❻ What is the total number of plants if there are 6 rows of 8 plants in one field and 4 rows of 7 plants in another?

_____

Square and Triangular Numbers

1 Find the following square numbers.

a. 2 squared = _____

b. 7 squared = _____

c. 5 squared = _____

d. 4 squared = _____

e. 6 × 6 = _____

f. 9 × 9 = _____

2 Find the following triangular numbers.

a. ∙ = _____

b. = _____

c. = _____

d. = _____

e. 1 + 2 + 3 + 4 + 5 = _____

f. 1 + 2 + 3 + 4 + 5 + 6 = _____

3 Complete the following table for triangular numbers.

	a.	b.	c.	d.	e.	f.	
Triangular Number Order	1	2	3	4	5	6	7
Triangular Number							28

4 Complete the following.

a. 9 = _____ squared

b. 1 = _____ squared

c. 64 = _____ squared

d. 100 = _____ squared

e. 25 = _____ squared

f. 36 = _____ squared

5 What is the tenth triangular number? _____

6 **a.** Draw 3 squared using dots.   **b.** Draw the 7th triangular number using dots.

Multiples

1 Which of the numbers 10, 12, 18, or 21 are multiples of:

    a. 2? _____   **b.** 5? _____   **c.** 6? _____

    d. 9? _____   **e.** 7? _____   **f.** 3? _____

2 True or false?

    a. 1 is a multiple of 3. _____   **b.** 12 is a multiple of 3. _____

    c. 36 is a multiple of 9. _____   **d.** 90 is a multiple of 10. _____

    e. 14 is a multiple of 6. _____   **f.** 20 is a multiple of 4. _____

3 Write the product of each pair of factors.

    a. 3 and 1 = _____   **b.** 5 and 3 = _____

    c. 9 and 2 = _____   **d.** 10 and 4 = _____

    e. 6 and 4 = _____   **f.** 4 and 7 = _____

4 Complete the following.

    a. 12 is a multiple of _____ and _____.   **b.** 10 is a multiple of _____ and _____.

    c. 35 is a multiple of _____ and _____.   **d.** 7 is a multiple of _____ and _____.

    e. 16 is a multiple of _____ and _____.   **f.** 32 is a multiple of _____ and _____.

5 **a.** Which of the numbers 14, 7, or 15 is a multiple of 5? _____

    b. True or false? 9 is a multiple of 3. _____

    c. The product of the factors 8 and 3 is _____.

    d. 20 is a multiple of _____ and _____.

6 List the first ten multiples of 4 and 8, and then circle those that they have in common.

    4: _____

    8: _____

Factors

1 Write one pair of factors for each number.

    a. 5 _____, _____   **b.** 13 _____, _____   **c.** 7 _____, _____

    d. 2 _____, _____   **e.** 11 _____, _____   **f.** 23 _____, _____

2 True or false?

    a. 4 is a factor of 32. _____   **b.** 1 is a factor of 11. _____

    c. 3 is a factor of 10. _____   **d.** 5 is a factor of 26. _____

    e. 6 is a factor of 42. _____   **f.** 7 is a factor of 27. _____

3 Write two pairs of factors for each number.

    a. 10 _____, _____; _____, _____   **b.** 20 _____, _____; _____, _____

    c. 8 _____, _____; _____, _____   **d.** 9 _____, _____; _____, _____

    e. 32 _____, _____; _____, _____   **f.** 4 _____, _____; _____, _____

4 List all the factors of the following numbers.

    a. 6: _____, _____, _____, _____

    b. 15: _____, _____, _____, _____

    c. 20: _____, _____, _____, _____, _____, _____

    d. 16: _____, _____, _____, _____, _____

    e. 12: _____, _____, _____, _____, _____, _____

    f. 24: _____, _____, _____, _____, _____, _____, _____, _____

5 Complete the table.

Factor	3	3			5	7
Factor	10	9	6	10		
Product			24	40	35	56

6 List all the factors of 36 and 18, and then circle those that they have in common.

    36: _____

    18: _____

1 Large multiplication equations can be split into tens and ones components, each calculated and added together. Complete the following using this strategy.

a. 16×5
$= (10 \times 5) + (6 \times 5)$

$=$ _____ + _____

$=$ _____

b. 19×6
$= (10 \times 6) + (9 \times 6)$

$=$ _____ + _____

$=$ _____

c. 14×8
$= (10 \times 8) + (\underline{} \times \underline{})$

$=$ _____ + _____

$=$ _____

2 Multiplying with tens is the same as normal multiplication except a zero is added to the answer (e.g., $5 \times 5 = 25$ and $5 \times 50 = 250$). Complete each of the following using this strategy.

a. $\begin{array}{r} 70 \\ \times 5 \\ \hline \end{array}$
b. $\begin{array}{r} 30 \\ \times 6 \\ \hline \end{array}$
c. $\begin{array}{r} 60 \\ \times 8 \\ \hline \end{array}$
d. $\begin{array}{r} 20 \\ \times 9 \\ \hline \end{array}$
e. $\begin{array}{r} 80 \\ \times 4 \\ \hline \end{array}$
f. $\begin{array}{r} 50 \\ \times 7 \\ \hline \end{array}$

3 Large multiplication equations can be split into smaller components when one of the factors is 2, so the concept of doubling can be used. Complete each of the following using this strategy.

a. 20×7

$= 2 \times 10 \times 7$

$= 2 \times$ _____

$=$ _____

b. 14×6

$= 2 \times 7 \times 6$

$= 2 \times$ _____

$=$ _____

c. 18×5

$= 2 \times \underline{} \times 5$

$= 2 \times$ _____

$=$ _____

4 Find the missing numbers.

a. $7 \times 10 =$ _____

b. $9 \times$ _____ $= 63$

c. _____ $\times 8 = 56$

d. $6 \times$ _____ $= 42$

e. _____ $\times 5 = 45$

f. $5 \times$ _____ $= 0$

5 Multiplying with hundreds is the same as normal multiplication, except two zeros are added to the answer, e.g., $5 \times 5 = 25$ and $5 \times 500 = 2,500$. Complete each of the following using this strategy.

a. $\begin{array}{r} 400 \\ \times 8 \\ \hline \end{array}$
b. $\begin{array}{r} 500 \\ \times 6 \\ \hline \end{array}$
c. $\begin{array}{r} 900 \\ \times 3 \\ \hline \end{array}$
d. $\begin{array}{r} 700 \\ \times 4 \\ \hline \end{array}$

6 Complete the factor tree by filling in the missing factors.

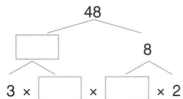

Multiplication by Tens

1 Find the value of the following.

    a. 6 tens = _____   **b.** 5 tens = _____

    c. 14 tens = _____   **d.** 18 tens = _____

    e. 72 tens = _____   **f.** 56 tens = _____

2 Multiply the following.

    a. $3 \times 10 =$ _____   **b.** $9 \times 10 =$ _____

    c. $12 \times 10 =$ _____   **d.** $17 \times 10 =$ _____

    e. $36 \times 10 =$ _____   **f.** $23 \times 10 =$ _____

3 Multiply the following by first breaking down the larger number into a smaller number times 10.

a. 8×20	**b.** 5×60	**c.** 7×30
$= 8 \times 2 \times 10$	$= 5 \times 6 \times 10$	$= 7 \times 3 \times 10$
= _____	= _____	= _____
d. 5×90	**e.** 4×40	**f.** 6×70
$= 5 \times 9 \times 10$	$= 4 \times 4 \times 10$	$= 6 \times 7 \times 10$
= _____	= _____	= _____

4 Multiply the following.

    a. $6 \times 60 =$ _____   **b.** $8 \times 80 =$ _____

    c. $4 \times 30 =$ _____   **d.** $7 \times 50 =$ _____

    e. $5 \times 60 =$ _____   **f.** $8 \times 60 =$ _____

5 Calculate each of the following.

    a. $30 \times 12 =$ _____   **b.** $60 \times 11 =$ _____   **c.** $50 \times 10 =$ _____

6 There are 81 rows of seats with 10 seats per row inside Theo's Theater. How many total seats are in the theater?

    _____

Extended Multiplication

1 Complete the multiplication patterns.

a. $2 \times 6 =$ _____   **b.** $3 \times 9 =$ _____   **c.** $5 \times 7 =$ _____   **d.** $9 \times 10 =$ _____

$20 \times 6 =$ _____ $30 \times 9 =$ _____ $50 \times 7 =$ _____ $90 \times 10 =$ _____

$200 \times 6 =$ _____ $300 \times 9 =$ _____ $500 \times 7 =$ _____ $900 \times 10 =$ _____

2 Multiply the following.

a. $\begin{array}{r} 32 \\ \times\ 4 \\ \hline \end{array}$ **b.** $\begin{array}{r} 41 \\ \times\ 5 \\ \hline \end{array}$ **c.** $\begin{array}{r} 53 \\ \times\ 6 \\ \hline \end{array}$

d. $\begin{array}{r} 65 \\ \times\ 6 \\ \hline \end{array}$ **e.** $\begin{array}{r} 26 \\ \times\ 4 \\ \hline \end{array}$ **f.** $\begin{array}{r} 36 \\ \times\ 7 \\ \hline \end{array}$

3 Large multiplication equations can be split into tens and ones components, each calculated and added together. Complete the following using this strategy.

a. 2×43 **b.** 4×83 **c.** 6×16 **d.** 4×53

$= (2 \times 40) + (2 \times 3)$ $= (4 \times 80) + (4 \times 3)$ $= (6 \times \underline{\ \ }) + (6 \times \underline{\ \ })$ $= (4 \times \underline{\ \ }) + (4 \times \underline{\ \ })$

$=$ _____ $+$ _____ $=$ _____ $+$ _____ $=$ _____ $+$ _____ $=$ _____ $+$ _____

$=$ _____ $=$ _____ $=$ _____ $=$ _____

4 Multiply the following.

a. $\begin{array}{r} 227 \\ \times\ \ \ 3 \\ \hline \end{array}$ **b.** $\begin{array}{r} 145 \\ \times\ \ \ 6 \\ \hline \end{array}$ **c.** $\begin{array}{r} 128 \\ \times\ \ \ 7 \\ \hline \end{array}$

d. $\begin{array}{r} 290 \\ \times\ \ \ 4 \\ \hline \end{array}$ **e.** $\begin{array}{r} 157 \\ \times\ \ \ 5 \\ \hline \end{array}$ **f.** $\begin{array}{r} 148 \\ \times\ \ \ 8 \\ \hline \end{array}$

5 Find the total number of bananas if there are 126 in each of 8 boxes. _____

6 Make up a multiplication word problem using the numbers 6 and 394, and then solve it.

_____

_____

_____

Division

❶ Use the multiplication equations to complete the division problems.

a. $5 \times 7 = 35$ **b.** $9 \times 8 = 72$ **c.** $6 \times 7 = 42$ **d.** $12 \times 4 = 48$

$7 \overline{)35}$ $9 \overline{)72}$ $6 \overline{)42}$ $4 \overline{)48}$

$5 \overline{)35}$ $8 \overline{)72}$ $7 \overline{)42}$ $12 \overline{)48}$

❷ Divide the following.

a. $7 \overline{)35}$ **b.** $3 \overline{)18}$ **c.** $2 \overline{)10}$

d. $8 \overline{)64}$ **e.** $10 \overline{)60}$ **f.** $6 \overline{)24}$

❸ Divide the following.

a. $54 \div 6 =$ _____   **b.** $45 \div 9 =$ _____

c. $48 \div 6 =$ _____   **d.** $16 \div 4 =$ _____

e. $68 \div 2 =$ _____   **f.** $96 \div 3 =$ _____

❹ Divide the following.

a. $2 \overline{)38}$ **b.** $8 \overline{)96}$ **c.** $5 \overline{)95}$

d. $6 \overline{)78}$ **e.** $3 \overline{)51}$ **f.** $3 \overline{)84}$

❺ How many baskets are needed for each situation?

a. 6 pineapples; 2 in each basket _____   **b.** 40 apples; 8 in each basket _____

c. 20 pears; 5 in each basket _____   **d.** 21 plums; 7 in each basket _____

e. 70 strawberries; 10 in each basket _____   **f.** 9 puppies; 3 in each basket _____

❻ **a.** How many groups of 6 are there in 36? _____

b. How many would there be in each share, if 63 are shared equally among 9? _____

c. How many different ways can you put 24 oranges into baskets, having the same number of oranges in each basket?

_____

1 Find the missing numbers.

  a. 1 × _____ = 5   **b.** 3 × _____ = 30   **c.** _____ × 9 = 27

  d. _____ × 3 = 24   **e.** _____ × 5 = 20   **f.** 4 × _____ = 32

2 Find each of the following.

  a. 6 apples shared by 3 people _____   **b.** 16 slices of bread shared by 8 moms _____

  c. 40 desks, 4 in each row, _____ rows   **d.** 56 cards, 7 in each row, _____ rows

  e. 14 days, how many weeks? _____   **f.** 36 months, how many years? _____

3 Write each as a number sentence, showing remainders.

  a. 15 shared among 4, equals 3 and remainder 3 _____

  b. 10 divided by 4, equals 2 and remainder 2 _____

  c. 24 shared among 7, equals 3 and remainder 3 _____

  d. 50 shared among 6, equals 8 and remainder 2 _____

  e. 100 divided by 9, equals 11 and remainder 1 _____

  f. 45 divided by 7, equals 6 and remainder 3 _____

4 Find each of the following. Show remainders.

  a. 32 carrots shared among 10 rabbits _____

  b. 20 CDs sorted into 3 piles _____

  c. 50 marbles shared among 8 boys _____

  d. 72 days, how many weeks? _____

5 Andrew saw several spiders. In all, Andrew counted
56 legs. How many spiders did he see?   _____

6 Draw a picture to show 33 divided by 5, and then solve it. _____

Division with Multiplication Grid

1 Complete the spaces labeled a.–f. on the grid.

x	0	1	2	3	4	5	6	7	8	9	10
0	0	0	0	0	0	0	0	0	0	0	0
1	0	1	2	3	4	5	6	7	8	9	10
2	0	2	4	6	8	10	12	14	16	18	20
3	0	3	6	9	12	15	18	21	24	**d.**	30
4	0	4	8	12	16	**b.**	24	28	32	36	40
5	0	5	10	15	20	25	30	35	40	45	50
6	0	6	12	**a.**	24	30	36	42	48	54	60
7	0	7	14	21	28	35	42	**c.**	56	63	70
8	0	8	16	24	32	40	48	56	64	**f.**	80
9	0	9	18	27	36	45	54	63	72	81	90
10	0	10	20	30	**e.**	50	60	70	80	90	100

a. _____

b. _____

c. _____

d. _____

e. _____

f. _____

2 Use the multiplication grid to answer the following.

a. $24 \div 6 =$ _____   **b.** $50 \div 5 =$ _____   **c.** $64 \div 8 =$ _____

d. $20 \div 10 =$ _____   **e.** $15 \div 3 =$ _____   **f.** $42 \div 6 =$ _____

3 Use the multiplication grid to complete the following.

a. $6\overline{)54}$ **b.** $7\overline{)70}$ **c.** $4\overline{)32}$

d. $8\overline{)48}$ **e.** $7\overline{)56}$ **f.** $2\overline{)16}$

4 Use the multiplication grid to fill in the spaces.

a. $27 \div$ _____ $= 9$ **b.** _____ $\div 5 = 5$ **c.** $81 \div$ _____ $= 9$

d. _____ $\div 3 = 8$ **e.** $28 \div$ _____ $= 7$ **f.** _____ $\div 4 = 5$

5 Janet is using a box of 49 beads to make necklaces. If Janet uses 7 beads for each necklace, how many necklaces can she make?

_____

6 Design a box that holds 24 apples. The apples must be arranged in equal rows. Draw one way of arranging the apples in the box.

Estimation with Division

1 Estimate each of the following in whole numbers.

    a. $62 \div 3 =$ _____

    b. $92 \div 5 =$ _____

    c. $71 \div 7 =$ _____

    d. $59 \div 5 =$ _____

    e. $81 \div 4 =$ _____

    f. $47 \div 7 =$ _____

2 Calculate the following and compare the answers to the estimations of question 1.

    a. $3\overline{)62}$

    b. $5\overline{)92}$

    c. $7\overline{)71}$

    d. $5\overline{)59}$

    e. $4\overline{)81}$

    f. $7\overline{)47}$

3 Estimate each of the following in whole numbers.

    a. $142 \div 7 =$ _____

    b. $297 \div 5 =$ _____

    c. $121 \div 6 =$ _____

    d. $352 \div 10 =$ _____

    e. $219 \div 4 =$ _____

    f. $332 \div 3 =$ _____

4 Estimate the answer to each of the following in whole numbers.

    a. Share 42 equally among 5. _____

    b. Divide 137 by 10. _____

    c. Divide 182 equally among 9. _____

    d. Find 49 divided by 4. _____

    e. How many groups of 6 are there in 29? _____

    f. How many threes are there in 35? _____

5 Amy, Joy, Ken, and John all earned a total of $79 for cleaning the neighborhood park.

    a. Estimate, to the nearest dollar, how much each person's share was. _____

    b. Write a number sentence for the above situation, and then solve it.

    _____

6 Draw 38 triangles and estimate (in a whole number) how many groups of 3 triangles there are. Then circle groups of 3 triangles to find the exact answer and remainder. Write the number sentence below.

    Estimate = _____   Number Sentence = _____

Division with Remainders

1 Find the answer and check it (using multiplication and addition) for each of the following division problems. The first one has been done for you.

a.

$$2\overline{)19} = 9\,r\,1$$
$$-18$$
$$\overline{1}$$

Check

$2 \times 9 = 18$
$+\,1$
$\overline{19}$

b.

$3\overline{)26}$

Check

c.

$4\overline{)38}$

Check

d.

$5\overline{)28}$

Check

e.

$6\overline{)29}$

Check

f.

$3\overline{)34}$

Check

2 Divide the following.

a. $2\overline{)43}$ **b.** $3\overline{)34}$ **c.** $4\overline{)13}$ **d.** $5\overline{)29}$ **e.** $7\overline{)60}$ **f.** $2\overline{)29}$

3 Divide the following.

a. $35 \div 2 = $ _____   **b.** $46 \div 4 = $ _____   **c.** $92 \div 9 = $ _____

d. $56 \div 5 = $ _____   **e.** $45 \div 6 = $ _____   **f.** $73 \div 7 = $ _____

4 At the horseback riding park, 9 horses are used for each riding session. How many riding sessions are needed if there are:

a. 20 children? _____   **b.** 50 children? _____

c. 35 children? _____   **d.** 59 children? _____

5 Solve the following, also writing how many are left over.

a. 32 bottles put into 6 rows. How many are there in each row? _____

b. 53 days. How many weeks are there? _____

c. 63 cows in herds of 10. How many herds are there? _____

d. 96 marbles in 9 groups. How many groups are there? _____

6 Sue Lin had 5 books left after she gave her friends 7 each. If she had 33 books to begin with, how many friends did she give books to? _____

Division Practice

❶ Use the first sentence to complete the second one.

a. $(5 \times 4) + 3 = 23$

$23 \div 4 =$ _____

b. $(3 \times 6) + 1 = 19$

$19 \div 6 =$ _____

c. $(2 \times 10) + 1 = 21$

$21 \div 10 =$ _____

d. $(6 \times 7) + 5 = 47$

$47 \div 7 =$ _____

e. $(8 \times 3) + 2 = 26$

$26 \div 3 =$ _____

f. $(9 \times 5) + 3 = 48$

$48 \div 5 =$ _____

❷ Divide the following.

a. $7 \overline{)3\,8}$

b. $5 \overline{)2\,7}$

c. $6 \overline{)3\,9}$

d. $9 \overline{)1\,0\,0}$

e. $2 \overline{)4\,1}$

f. $3 \overline{)3\,8}$

❸ Divide the following.

a. $36 \div 2 =$ _____

b. $45 \div 3 =$ _____

c. $51 \div 3 =$ _____

d. $68 \div 4 =$ _____

e. $85 \div 5 =$ _____

f. $92 \div 4 =$ _____

❹ Complete each path.

a. $70 \div 7$ ⟶ _____ x 3 ⟶ _____ ÷ 5 ⟶ _____ x 3 ⟶ _____

b. $64 \div 8$ ⟶ _____ x 2 ⟶ _____ ÷ 4 ⟶ _____ x 10 ⟶ _____

c. $66 \div 6$ ⟶ _____ x 3 ⟶ _____ ÷ 3 ⟶ _____ x 1 ⟶ _____

d. $45 \div 9$ ⟶ _____ x 10 ⟶ _____ x 2 ⟶ _____ ÷ 10 ⟶ _____

❺ Divide the following.

a. $3 \overline{)9\,2}$

b. $5 \overline{)7\,1}$

c. $7 \overline{)7\,4}$

❻ Judy's mom cooked 29 chicken nuggets for Judy and 5 of her friends to eat. If each person will eat the same number of chicken nuggets, how many will each person eat? How many will be left over?

_____

1 Write one multiplication fact and one division fact for each set of numbers in the triangles.

a. 35 / 5 7 _____

b. 30 / 3 10 _____

c. 56 / 8 7 _____

d. 72 / 9 8 _____

e. 16 / 8 2 _____

f. 4 / 4 1 _____

2 Find the missing numbers.

a. $4 \times _____ = 8$

b. $6 \times _____ = 18$

c. $2 \times _____ = 20$

d. $_____ \times 6 = 24$

e. $_____ \times 9 = 63$

f. $_____ \times 10 = 80$

3 Divide the following.

a. $5\overline{)85}$ **b.** $3\overline{)72}$ **c.** $4\overline{)60}$ **d.** $6\overline{)78}$ **e.** $3\overline{)81}$ **f.** $7\overline{)84}$

4 Find the number sentence and answer to each of the following.

a. Helen had 8 chickens in each of 6 pens. How many chickens were there altogether?

_____

b. Bill divided 98 nails into 7 boxes. How many nails were there in each box?

_____

c. Albert had 5 piles of 9 cards. How many cards were there altogether?

_____

d. A family ate 84 biscuits in 1 week. How many biscuits were eaten each day?

_____

5 Paul bought 2 bags of avocados for $6 each. There were 3 avocados in each bag.

a. How much did he pay for the avocados altogether? _____

b. How much did each avocado cost? _____

6 Fill in the missing numbers on the path.

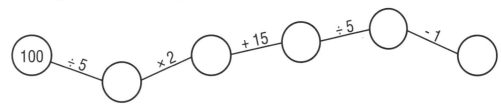

Inverse Operations

1 Check the addition facts with subtraction, and write *true* or *false*. The first one has been done for you.

a. 49 + 21 = 60 ___false___

60 − __21__ = __39__

b. 57 + 18 = 75 _____

75 − _____ = _____

c. 36 + 16 = 52 _____

52 − _____ = _____

d. 84 + 27 = 101 _____

101 − _____ = _____

e. 63 + 29 = 92 _____

92 − _____ = _____

f. 58 + 37 = 95 _____

95 − _____ = _____

2 Check the subtraction fact with addition, and write *true* or *false*.

a. 43 − 26 = 17 _____

b. 53 − 14 = 29 _____

c. 71 − 21 = 60 _____

d. 85 − 27 = 58 _____

e. 35 − 18 = 17 _____

f. 90 − 26 = 74 _____

3 Write a division fact from the following multiplication equations.

a. 12 × 5 = 60

60 ÷ _____ = _____

b. 14 × 7 = 98

98 ÷ _____ = _____

c. 16 × 3 = 48

48 ÷ _____ = _____

d. 15 × 12 = 180

180 ÷ _____ = _____

e. 9 × 16 = 144

144 ÷ _____ = _____

f. 18 × 8 = 144

144 ÷ _____ = _____

4 Write a multiplication fact from each division equation.

a. 96 ÷ 4 = 24

_____ × _____ = 96

b. 108 ÷ 12 = 9

_____ × _____ = 108

c. 78 ÷ 13 = 6

_____ × _____ = 78

d. 126 ÷ 14 = 9

_____ × _____ = 126

e. 105 ÷ 7 = 15

_____ × _____ = 105

f. 132 ÷ 4 = 33

_____ × _____ = 132

5 Find the mistakes in the following problems and correct them.

a.
```
   4 9
×    2
-------
   8 8
```

b.
```
      6 4
3 ) 1 3 2
```

6 Molly had 23 hair ribbons. After opening her birthday gifts, Molly now has 37 hair ribbons. Write the equation and solve it to show how many hair ribbons Molly got for her birthday.

_____

Number Lines

① On the number line, write the values of each of the labeled points a–f.

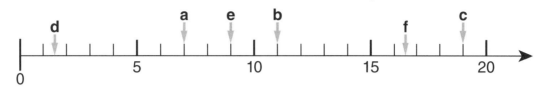

a. _____   b. _____   c. _____

d. _____   e. _____   f. _____

② Use the number line to solve the addition equations by "jumping" up the number line by tens and ones.

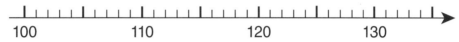

a. 109 + 19 = _____   b. 105 + 17 = _____   c. 116 + 14 = _____

d. 103 + 18 = _____   e. 102 + 26 = _____   f. 107 + 14 = _____

③ Use the number line to solve the subtraction equations by "jumping" down the number line by tens and ones.

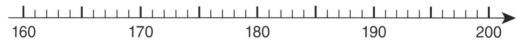

a. 196 − 17 = _____   b. 185 − 18 = _____   c. 182 − 14 = _____

d. 200 − 18 = _____   e. 191 − 13 = _____   f. 186 − 19 = _____

④ Use the number line to complete the following multiplication and division equations.

a. 5 × 6 = _____   b. 2 × 15 = _____   c. 2 × 12 = _____

d. 20 ÷ 2 = _____   e. 24 ÷ 6 = _____   f. 26 ÷ 2 = _____

⑤ On the number line, write the values of each of the labeled points a–d.

a. _____   b. _____   c. _____   d. _____

⑥ Draw a number line from 20 to 30 that includes the following numbers labeled.

a. 21

b. $26\frac{1}{4}$

c. $23\frac{1}{2}$

d. $29\frac{3}{4}$

Prime and Composite Numbers

1 Find the factors of the following numbers.

    a. 7 _____

    b. 11 _____

    c. 17 _____

    d. 5 _____

    e. 23 _____

    f. 31 _____

2 True or false?

    a. 7 is a prime number. _____

    b. 2 is a composite number. _____

    c. 41 is a prime number. _____

    d. 15 is a composite number. _____

    e. 47 is a composite number. _____

    f. 21 is a prime number. _____

3 Find all the factors of the following numbers.

    a. 4 _____

    b. 8 _____

    c. 12 _____

    d. 52 _____

    e. 18 _____

    f. 20 _____

4 Label each of the following numbers as *prime* or *composite*.

    a. 29 _____

    b. 43 _____

    c. 35 _____

    d. 49 _____

    e. 56 _____

    f. 37 _____

5 **a.** What type of numbers are all of the numbers in question 1? _____

    b. What type of numbers are all of the numbers in question 3? _____

6 Find all the prime numbers between 100 and 110.

_____

1-Step and 2-Step Rules

❶ Continue each pattern by following the rule.

   a. Add 5:   20, _____, _____, _____

   b. Add 8:   50, _____, _____, _____

   c. Multiply by 2:   5, _____, _____, _____

   d. Multiply by 3:   1, _____, _____, _____

   e. Subtract 9:   100, _____, _____, _____

   f. Divide by 4:   64, _____, _____, _____

❷ Write the next number in each pattern.

   a. 1, 5, 25, _____   **b.** 103, 100, 97, _____

   c. 4, 8, 16, _____   **d.** 400, 200, 100, _____

   e. 10, 21, 32, _____   **f.** 1, 5, 9, _____

❸ Write the rule for each pattern from question 2.

   a. _____   **b.** _____

   c. _____   **d.** _____

   e. _____   **f.** _____

❹ These patterns have 2 steps in each rule. Both steps must be done to get to the next number. Write the next three terms in each pattern.

   a. Rule: $\times 3 + 1$ **b.** Rule: $\times 10 - 5$

      1, 4, _____, _____, _____   1, 5, _____, _____, _____

   c. Rule: $+ 10 - 3$ **d.** Rule: $- 1 + 5$

      10, 17, _____, _____, _____   10, 14, _____, _____, _____

❺ Find the 2-step rule for the pattern below and give the next number.

   2; 12; 62; 312; 1,562; _____   Rule: _____

❻ **a.** Make up a simple 2-step rule for a pattern. _____

   b. Write the first five numbers in this pattern starting with the number 10.

      10, _____, _____, _____, _____

Calculator Addition and Subtraction

❶ Use a calculator to add the following.

a. 88 + 19 = _____

b. 466 + 55 = _____

c. 698 + 49 = _____

d. 325 + 1,649 = _____

e. 8,752 + 11,056 = _____

f. 3,261 + 2,054 = _____

❷ Use a calculator to subtract the following.

a. 231 – 186 = _____

b. 80 – 29 = _____

c. 421 – 396 = _____

d. 3,562 – 1,079 = _____

e. 24,681 – 3,421 = _____

f. 3,498 – 2,999 = _____

❸ Use a calculator to double each of the following.

a. 98 _____

b. 89 _____

c. 146 _____

d. 64 _____

e. 521 _____

f. 3,426 _____

❹ Use a calculator to find half of each of the following.

a. 592 _____

b. 706 _____

c. 326 _____

d. 418 _____

e. 1,528 _____

f. 1,988 _____

❺ If you start with 1,024, how many times does it need to be halved (divided by 2) to reach 1? List the numbers below.

_____

_____

❻ If you start with 6, how many times does it need to be doubled to reach 3,072? List the numbers below.

_____

_____

Calculator Multiplication and Division

1 Use a calculator to multiply the following.

a. 4 × 60 = _____   b. 8 × 90 = _____

c. 7 × 70 = _____   d. 40 × 20 = _____

e. 70 × 30 = _____   f. 40 × 50 = _____

2 Use a calculator to divide the following.

a. 360 ÷ 2 = _____   b. 840 ÷ 60 = _____

c. 940 ÷ 5 = _____   d. 940 ÷ 2 = _____

e. 960 ÷ 6 = _____   f. 560 ÷ 8 = _____

3 Use a calculator to multiply the following.

a. 49 × 21 = _____   b. 68 × 35 = _____

c. 28 × 87 = _____   d. 92 × 56 = _____

e. 125 × 32 = _____   f. 259 × 68 = _____

4 Use a calculator to divide the following.

a. 150 ÷ 6 = _____   b. 203 ÷ 7 = _____

c. 423 ÷ 9 = _____   d. 234 ÷ 78 = _____

e. 1,470 ÷ 15 = _____   f. 1,150 ÷ 46 = _____

5 Use a calculator to complete the following patterns.

a.	Multiply by 14	2	28		
b.	Multiply by 21	3	63		
c.	Divide by 8	4,096	512		

6 Use a calculator to complete the following path.

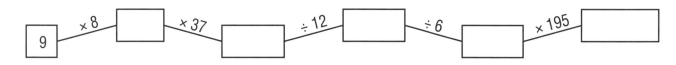

Fraction Names

1 What fraction of each shape is shaded?

a.  _____

b. 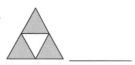 _____

c. 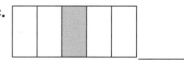 _____

d. 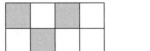 _____

e. 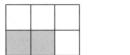 _____

f. 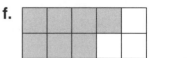 _____

2 What fraction of each shape in question 1 is **not** shaded?

a. _____

b. _____

c. _____

d. _____

e. _____

f. _____

3 Shade part of each shape to match the given fraction.

a. $\frac{1}{4}$

b. $\frac{6}{10}$

c. $\frac{2}{5}$

d. $\frac{3}{10}$

e. $\frac{4}{5}$

f. $\frac{3}{4}$

4 Write *true* or *false* for each statement.

a. $1 = \frac{4}{4}$ _____

b. $\frac{5}{8} = 1$ _____

c. $\frac{9}{10} = 1$ _____

d. $\frac{3}{4}$ is less than $\frac{3}{8}$ _____

e. $\frac{1}{10}$ is less than $\frac{1}{5}$ _____

f. $\frac{1}{4}$ is less than $\frac{1}{3}$ _____

5 Write each of the following fractions in words.

a. $\frac{1}{4}$ _____

b. $\frac{2}{5}$ _____

c. $\frac{3}{10}$ _____

d. $\frac{1}{8}$ _____

e. $\frac{1}{2}$ _____

f. $\frac{3}{4}$ _____

6 Name the fraction of each group that is shaded.

a. _____

b.  _____

c. ⬤⬤⬤⬤◯◯◯◯ _____

1 Place each of the following fractions on the number line.

0   1   2

a. $\frac{1}{2}$ b. $1\frac{1}{4}$ c. $\frac{3}{4}$ d. $1\frac{1}{2}$ e. $\frac{1}{4}$ f. $1\frac{3}{4}$

2 Shade the fraction of each shape.

a. $\frac{1}{2}$ b. $\frac{3}{4}$ c. $\frac{2}{5}$

d. $\frac{5}{8}$ e. $\frac{1}{4}$ f. $\frac{3}{10}$

3 Shade part of each group to match the given fraction.

a. $\frac{1}{2}$ of the circles ○ ○ ○ ○ ○ ○   b. $\frac{5}{8}$ of the squares

c. $\frac{1}{4}$ of the triangles △ △ △ △   d. $\frac{3}{5}$ of the diamonds ◇ ◇ ◇ ◇ ◇

e. $\frac{7}{10}$ of the stars ☆ ☆ ☆ ☆ ☆ ☆ ☆ ☆ ☆ ☆   f. $\frac{7}{8}$ of the rectangles

4 Order the fractions from least to greatest.

a. $\frac{2}{8}, \frac{5}{8}, \frac{1}{8}, \frac{7}{8}$ _____

b. $\frac{4}{5}, \frac{2}{5}, \frac{3}{5}, \frac{1}{5}$ _____

c. $\frac{1}{10}, \frac{3}{10}, \frac{4}{10}, \frac{2}{10}$ _____

5 Order the fractions from greatest to least.

a. $\frac{9}{10}, \frac{6}{10}, \frac{4}{10}, \frac{8}{10}$ _____

b. $\frac{3}{4}, \frac{2}{4}, \frac{1}{4}, \frac{4}{4}$ _____

c. $\frac{1}{2}, \frac{1}{10}, \frac{1}{5}, \frac{4}{10}$ _____

6 Draw and shade shapes to show the following fractions.

a. $1\frac{3}{4}$ squares   b. $2\frac{4}{5}$ rectangles   c. $3\frac{1}{2}$ circles

Comparing Fractions

❶ Circle the larger fraction.

a. $\frac{1}{5}$ or $\frac{1}{4}$

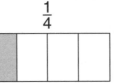

b. $\frac{1}{2}$ or $\frac{3}{4}$

 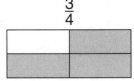

c. $\frac{1}{8}$ or $\frac{1}{10}$

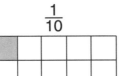

d. $\frac{1}{4}$ or $\frac{1}{8}$

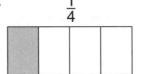 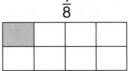

e. $\frac{6}{8}$ or $\frac{4}{10}$

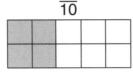

f. $\frac{4}{10}$ or $\frac{3}{5}$

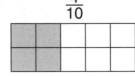 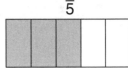

❷ Write *true* or *false* for each statement.

a. $1 = \frac{2}{2}$ _____

b. $\frac{7}{8} = 1$ _____

c. $1 = \frac{5}{5}$ _____

d. $1 = \frac{6}{8}$ _____

e. $\frac{9}{10} = 1$ _____

f. $\frac{4}{4} = 1$ _____

❸ Order the fractions from greatest to least.

a. $\frac{2}{5}, \frac{3}{5}, \frac{1}{5}, \frac{4}{5}$ _____

b. $\frac{3}{8}, \frac{5}{8}, \frac{4}{8}, \frac{1}{8}$ _____

c. $\frac{2}{10}, \frac{6}{10}, \frac{3}{10}, \frac{9}{10}$ _____

❹ Order the fractions from least to greatest.

a. $\frac{8}{10}, \frac{7}{10}, \frac{9}{10}, \frac{6}{10}$ _____

b. $\frac{1}{2}, \frac{3}{4}, 1, \frac{1}{4}$ _____

c. $\frac{7}{8}, 1, \frac{5}{8}, \frac{6}{8}$ _____

❺ Circle the smaller fraction.

a. $\frac{1}{10}$ or $\frac{1}{8}$

b. $\frac{1}{4}$ or $\frac{1}{5}$

c. $\frac{1}{2}$ or $\frac{1}{1}$

d. $\frac{1}{8}$ or $\frac{1}{5}$

e. $\frac{1}{2}$ or $\frac{1}{4}$

f. $\frac{1}{5}$ or $\frac{1}{10}$

❻ **a.** Which is larger: one-quarter or one-third? _____

b. Draw a diagram to support your answer.

Equivalent Fractions

❶ Shade and write an equivalent fraction for the one given.

a. $\frac{1}{2} = \frac{\square}{4}$

b. $\frac{1}{2} = \frac{\square}{8}$

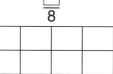

c. $\frac{1}{2} = \frac{\square}{10}$

d. $\frac{3}{5} = \frac{\square}{10}$

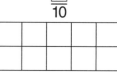

e. $\frac{4}{5} = \frac{\square}{10}$

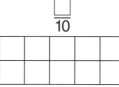

f. $\frac{3}{4} = \frac{\square}{8}$

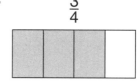 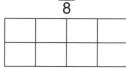

❷ True or false?

a. $\frac{1}{2} = \frac{3}{4}$ _____

b. $\frac{4}{5} = \frac{8}{10}$ _____

c. $\frac{3}{8} = \frac{6}{4}$ _____

d. $\frac{2}{2} = 1$ _____

e. $\frac{6}{10} = \frac{3}{5}$ _____

f. $\frac{2}{8} = \frac{3}{4}$ _____

❸ Write the equivalent fraction for the following fractions.

a. $\frac{4}{8} = \frac{\square}{2}$ **b.** $\frac{6}{10} = \frac{\square}{5}$ **c.** $\frac{1}{2} = \frac{\square}{10}$ **d.** $\frac{4}{10} = \frac{\square}{5}$ **e.** $\frac{6}{8} = \frac{\square}{4}$ **f.** $\frac{2}{8} = \frac{\square}{4}$

❹ Use the number line to help find the equivalent fractions. Give the number of:

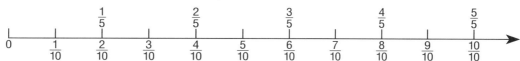

a. tenths in one-fifth. _____ **b.** tenths in two-fifths. _____ **c.** tenths in three-fifths. _____

d. tenths in four-fifths. _____ **e.** tenths in five-fifths. _____ **f.** fifths in four-tenths. _____

❺ Use the number line to help find the equivalent fractions. Give the number of:

a. eighths in $\frac{1}{2}$. _____ **b.** eighths in $\frac{3}{4}$. _____

c. eighths in $\frac{1}{4}$. _____ **d.** eighths in 1 whole. _____

❻ Draw a picture to represent $\frac{5}{8}$.

Mixed Numbers

❶ What fraction is shaded in each of the following diagrams?

a.  _____

b. 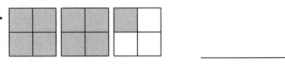 _____

c. 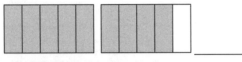 _____

d. 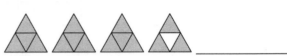 _____

e. 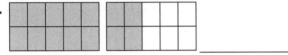 _____

f. 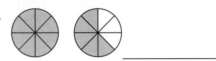 _____

❷ Complete the number lines.

a.

b.

c.

d.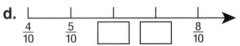

e.

f.

❸ Shade the shapes to show the mixed numbers.

a. $1\frac{1}{4}$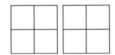

b. $1\frac{5}{8}$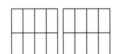

c. $1\frac{7}{10}$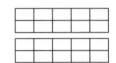

d. $1\frac{3}{5}$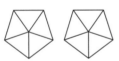

e. $1\frac{6}{8}$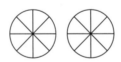

f. $1\frac{3}{4}$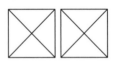

❹ Circle the larger mixed number in each pair.

a. $1\frac{2}{5}$ $1\frac{3}{5}$

b. $1\frac{2}{10}$ $1\frac{9}{10}$

c. $2\frac{3}{4}$ $1\frac{1}{2}$

❺ Circle the smaller value in each pair.

a. $1\frac{5}{10}$ 2

b. $3\frac{1}{4}$ $2\frac{3}{4}$

c. $1\frac{8}{10}$ $2\frac{1}{10}$

❻ **a.** Draw a diagram to show $3\frac{5}{8}$.

b. How many eighths are there shaded altogether? _____

❶ What fraction of each hundreds square is shaded?

a.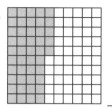

b.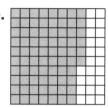

c.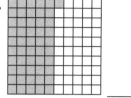

d.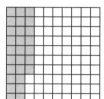

e.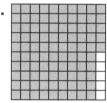

f.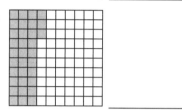

❷ What fraction of each hundreds square in question 1 is **not** shaded?

a. _____   **b.** _____   **c.** _____

d. _____   **e.** _____   **f.** _____

❸ Shade part of each hundreds square to match the given fraction.

a. $\frac{13}{100}$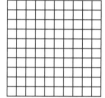

b. $\frac{67}{100}$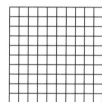

c. $\frac{100}{100}$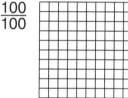

d. $\frac{72}{100}$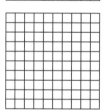

e. $\frac{89}{100}$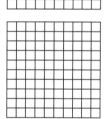

f. $\frac{26}{100}$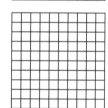

❹ Write each of the following as a decimal.

a. five-hundredths _____   **b.** sixty-two hundredths _____

c. nineteen-hundredths _____   **d.** nine-hundredths _____

e. forty-hundredths _____   **f.** eighty-five hundredths _____

❺ Label each of the following decimals on the number line.

a. 0.25   **b.** 0.75

c. 0.39   **d.** 0.05

e. 0.90   **f.** 0.10

❻ How many cents are in each of the following amounts?

a. $2.90 _____   **b.** $1.75 _____   **c.** $5.05 _____

Tenths

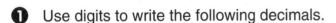

1 Use digits to write the following decimals.

    a. six-tenths _____   **b.** nine-tenths _____

    c. four-tenths _____   **d.** two-tenths _____

    e. one-tenth _____   **f.** seven-tenths _____

2 Write the decimal for each of the following.

    a. $\frac{3}{10}$ _____   **b.** $\frac{5}{10}$ _____   **c.** $\frac{8}{10}$ _____

    d. $1\frac{4}{10}$ _____   **e.** $2\frac{1}{10}$ _____   **f.** $1\frac{6}{10}$ _____

3 Match each fraction with the correct decimal.

    a. $1\frac{1}{10}$ 0.2

    b. $\frac{5}{10}$ 0.3

    c. $\frac{2}{10}$ 1

    d. $\frac{10}{10}$ 1.1

    e. $1\frac{7}{10}$ 1.7

    f. $\frac{3}{10}$ 0.5

4 Use <, >, or = to make each of the following statements true.

    a. 0.2 ☐ 0.5   **b.** 0.3 ☐ 0.30   **c.** 0.6 ☐ 0.5

    d. 0.9 ☐ 1.0   **e.** 0.9 ☐ 0.1   **f.** 0.70 ☐ 0.7

5 Charlie was practicing shooting free throws in basketball practice. Out of ten free-throw attempts, Charlie made seven free throws.

    a. Write the decimal that shows the portion of free throws that Charlie made. _____

    b. Write the decimal that shows the portion of free throws that Charlie missed. _____

6 There are 100 centimeters in 1 meter. How many centimeters are in each of the following?

    a. 1.43 m _____   **b.** 2.59 m _____   **c.** 8.50 m _____

Decimals — Place Value

① Shade part of each hundreds square to match the given decimal.

a. 0.05 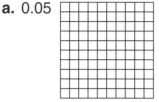 **b.** 0.80 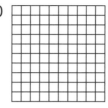 **c.** 0.72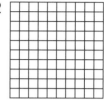

② Write the decimal that is shaded on each hundreds square.

a.  _____ **b.** 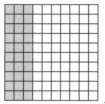 _____ **c.**  _____

③ Give the value of the 5 in each of the following numbers.

a. 1.56 _____   **b.** 5.21 _____

c. 3.05 _____   **d.** 1.15 _____

e. 6.50 _____   **f.** 15.92 _____

④ Write each of the following decimals in words.

a. 0.18 _____

b. 0.46 _____

c. 0.02 _____

d. 0.30 _____

⑤ Write each marked value as a decimal.

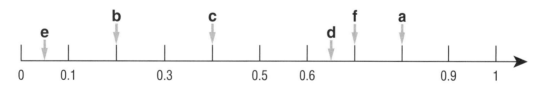

a. _____   **b.** _____   **c.** _____

d. _____   **e.** _____   **f.** _____

⑥ Complete the table.

Decimal	Fraction	Words	Diagram
0.4			
0.8			

Decimals

1 What decimal is shaded on each hundreds square?

a. 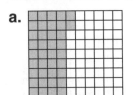 _____

b. _____

c. _____

d. 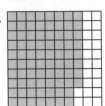 _____

e. 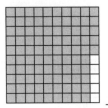 _____

f. _____

2 Circle the largest decimal in each of the following groups.

a. 0.26   0.78   0.43

b. 0.75   0.57   0.67

c. 0.39   0.93   0.65

3 Circle the smallest decimal in each of the following groups.

a. 0.10   0.03   0.16

b. 0.40   0.51   0.63

c. 0.29   0.36   0.17

4 Write the fraction in decimal form.

a. 6 tenths and 4 hundredths _____

b. 4 tenths and 2 hundredths _____

c. 9 tenths and 3 hundredths _____

d. 0 tenths and 1 hundredth _____

e. 5 tenths and 7 hundredths _____

f. 0 tenths and 2 hundredths _____

5 Give the value of each of the underlined digits.

a. 12.<u>3</u>0 _____

b. 0.<u>4</u>3 _____

c. 10.2<u>1</u> _____

d. <u>3</u>.65 _____

e. 1<u>1</u>.91 _____

f. 0.0<u>5</u> _____

6 Place each of the following numbers in the chart.

	H	T	O	.	Tths	Hths
a. 12.40						
b. 613.05						
c. 205.66						
d. 310.95						

Comparing Decimals

❶ Circle the greater decimal in each pair.

    a. 0.42   0.24   **b.** 0.92   0.15

    c. 0.46   0.66   **d.** 0.17   0.07

    e. 0.13   0.15   **f.** 0.40   0.44

❷ Write the next decimal in each of the patterns.

    a. 0.11, 0.12, _____   **b.** 0.56, 0.57, _____

    c. 0.81, 0.82, _____   **d.** 0.03, 0.04, _____

    e. 0.77, 0.78, _____   **f.** 0.38, 0.39, _____

❸ Order each set of decimals from least to greatest.

    a. 0.11, 0.19, 0.16, 0.14 _____

    b. 0.15, 0.05, 0.50, 0.45 _____

    c. 1.21, 1.28, 1.27, 1.23 _____

    d. 1.46, 2.38, 1.79, 3.66 _____

❹ Round each decimal to the nearest whole number.

    a. 1.13 _____   **b.** 6.75 _____

    c. 2.34 _____   **d.** 2.58 _____

    e. 2.98 _____   **f.** 0.86 _____

❺ Round each decimal to the nearest tenth.

    a. 4.21 _____   **b.** 4.58 _____

    c. 4.26 _____   **d.** 4.14 _____

❻ Write the next five numbers in a pattern starting at 0.5 and counting by 0.1.

    0.5, _____ , _____ , _____ , _____ , _____

Decimals with Whole Numbers

1 Write each of the following in decimal form.

    a. 1 and 36 hundredths _____   **b.** 1 and 19 hundredths _____

    c. 1 and 27 hundredths _____   **d.** 1 and 85 hundredths _____

    e. 5 and 6 hundredths _____   **f.** 5 and 90 hundredths _____

2 Match each fraction with the correct decimal.

    a. $1\frac{60}{100}$ 1.91

    b. $1\frac{16}{100}$ 3.21

    c. $1\frac{91}{100}$ 2.05

    d. $3\frac{21}{100}$ 1.6

    e. $2\frac{5}{100}$ 1.5

    f. $1\frac{50}{100}$ 1.16

3 Round each of the following decimals to the nearest whole number.

    a. 1.46 _____   **b.** 1.09 _____   **c.** 1.98 _____

    d. 1.73 _____   **e.** 1.55 _____   **f.** 1.72 _____

4 Order each set of decimals from least to greatest.

    a. 1.63, 1.76, 1.82, 1.31 _____

    b. 2.22, 2.32, 2.12, 2.42 _____

    c. 19.63, 20.58, 17.62, 14.32 _____

5 Order each set of decimals from greatest to least.

    a. 1.08, 1.11, 1.05, 1.10 _____

    b. 2.76, 2.39, 2.41, 2.58 _____

    c. 25.01, 25.63. 25.28, 25.91 _____

6 Draw a diagram to represent 1.47.

Fractions and Decimals

❶ Match each decimal with the correct fraction.

a. 1.09

b. 2.48

c. 1.90

d. 3.96

e. 1.19

f. 2.84

$1\frac{90}{100}$

$3\frac{96}{100}$

$1\frac{19}{100}$

$1\frac{9}{100}$

$2\frac{84}{100}$

$2\frac{48}{100}$

❷ Write the decimal for the following.

a. $\frac{6}{10}$ _____

b. $\frac{2}{10}$ _____

c. $\frac{49}{100}$ _____

d. $\frac{52}{100}$ _____

e. $1\frac{89}{100}$ _____

f. $2\frac{13}{100}$ _____

❸ Use decimals to write the following.

a. eight-tenths _____

b. three-tenths _____

c. 22 hundredths _____

d. 75 hundredths _____

e. one and nine-hundredths _____

f. three and thirty-five hundredths _____

❹ Circle the value that is greater in each pair.

a. $\frac{85}{100}$ or   0.89

b. $\frac{6}{10}$ or   0.8

c. $\frac{5}{10}$ or   0.3

❺ Circle the value that is less in each pair.

a. $\frac{47}{100}$ or   0.26

b. $1\frac{1}{10}$ or   1.15

c. $\frac{17}{100}$ or   1.70

❻ Tom has 245 cents in his piggy bank, and Sally has $2.54 in hers.

a. Who has more money? _____

b. What is the difference between the two amounts? _____

Decimal Addition

1 Add the decimals. Be sure to keep the numbers aligned.

a. Ones.Tenths

```
   4.7
+  1.2
```

b. Ones.Tenths

```
   2.6
+  1.3
```

c. Ones.Tenths

```
   1.1
+  1.2
```

d. Ones.Tenths

```
   3.2
+  1.7
```

e. Ones.Tenths

```
   4.2
+  1.3
```

f. Ones.Tenths

```
   2.3
+  3.5
```

2 Add the decimals.

a.
```
  4.69
+ 2.53
```

b.
```
  7.81
+ 1.52
```

c.
```
  3.79
+ 2.48
```

d.
```
  4.96
+ 1.37
```

e.
```
  3.75
+ 2.18
```

f.
```
  7.50
+ 1.56
```

3 Add the decimals.

a. 1.37 + 4.12 = _____

b. 3.58 + 2.31 = _____

c. 6.45 + 2.04 = _____

d. 1.71 + 4.18 = _____

4 Add the following amounts.

a.
```
  $2.75
+ $3.86
```

b.
```
  $2.81
+ $3.79
```

c.
```
  $2.99
+ $3.98
```

d.
```
  $7.65
+ $2.15
```

e.
```
  $4.19
+ $3.75
```

f.
```
  $2.55
+ $6.27
```

5 Add the following.

a.
```
  1.04
  3.22
+ 2.58
```

b.
```
  4.2
  1.2
+ 2.35
```

c.
```
  22.16
  25.75
+ 17.15
```

6 Tyler rode his bike 2.47 miles from his house to the library. After he finished, Tyler rode 1.65 miles from the library to his grandma's house. How many miles did Tyler ride his bike altogether?

_____

Decimal Subtraction

1 Subtract the decimals.

a. 4.63
    − 2.15

b. 4.77
    − 3.48

c. 2.14
    − 1.76

d. 8.52
    − 6.79

e. 7.35
    − 5.66

f. 5.26
    − 3.17

2 Subtract the decimals.

a. 2.48 − 1.46 = _____

b. 4.68 − 2.05 = _____

c. 1.85 − 0.63 = _____

d. 10.47 − 5.25 = _____

3 Subtract the following amounts.

a. $6.72
    − $4.23

b. $4.92
    − $3.91

c. $7.29
    − $4.56

d. $5.00
    − $3.22

e. $5.43
    − $2.90

f. $8.27
    − $4.30

4 Find the difference between the following measurements.

a. 5.29 gallons and 4.15 gallons _____

b. 6.35 feet and 3.21 feet _____

c. 9.65 miles and 7.50 miles _____

d. 5.87 pounds and 3.75 pounds _____

5 Find the price difference between the following menu items.

Hamburger combo	$7.25
Hamburger	$3.15
French fries	$2.50
Medium drink	$1.90
Apple slices	$1.75

a. Hamburger and Medium drink _____

b. French fries and Apple slices _____

c. Hamburger combo and Hamburger _____

d. Medium drink and Apple slices _____

6 The puppy weighed 10.45 lbs. and the kitten weighed
6.76 lbs. How much heavier was the puppy? _____

Decimal Addition and Subtraction

1 Add the decimals.

a. $\begin{array}{r} 6.31 \\ +2.38 \\ \hline \end{array}$

b. $\begin{array}{r} 3.54 \\ +4.37 \\ \hline \end{array}$

c. $\begin{array}{r} 9.06 \\ +0.59 \\ \hline \end{array}$

d. $\begin{array}{r} 1.29 \\ +3.08 \\ \hline \end{array}$

e. $\begin{array}{r} 5.14 \\ +3.67 \\ \hline \end{array}$

f. $\begin{array}{r} 0.72 \\ +3.69 \\ \hline \end{array}$

2 Subtract the decimals.

a. $\begin{array}{r} 6.54 \\ -1.23 \\ \hline \end{array}$

b. $\begin{array}{r} 7.95 \\ -2.64 \\ \hline \end{array}$

c. $\begin{array}{r} 5.87 \\ -1.95 \\ \hline \end{array}$

d. $\begin{array}{r} 2.46 \\ -1.91 \\ \hline \end{array}$

e. $\begin{array}{r} 9.76 \\ -3.28 \\ \hline \end{array}$

f. $\begin{array}{r} 7.95 \\ -2.99 \\ \hline \end{array}$

3 Find the following.

a. 3.14 − 2.11 = _____

b. 4.68 + 2.30 = _____

c. 4.93 + 6.05 = _____

d. 2.46 − 2.41 = _____

4 **a.** In the shopping cart, there were 1.5 pounds of grapes and 2.1 pounds of bananas. What was the total weight of fruit in the cart? _____

b. What is the difference in cost between two toys if one is $12.75 and the other is $10.49? _____

c. What was the total length of three pieces of wood: 1.75 ft., 2.51 ft., and 1.30 ft.? _____

5 Find the sum of the following numbers. Write your answer in digits.

three and seventeen-hundredths

two and five-hundredths

six and twenty-two hundredths   Sum = _____

6 Find the difference between the following numbers. Write your answer in digits.

seven and eighty-four hundredths

four and sixty-five hundredths   Difference = _____

Decimal Multiplication and Division (Calculator)

❶ Use a calculator to multiply the following decimals.

a. $0.65 \times 10 =$ _____

b. $0.23 \times 10 =$ _____

c. $0.49 \times 10 =$ _____

d. $1.78 \times 10 =$ _____

e. $4.07 \times 10 =$ _____

f. $7.32 \times 10 =$ _____

❷ Use a calculator to multiply the following decimals.

a. $0.17 \times 100 =$ _____

b. $0.55 \times 100 =$ _____

c. $0.82 \times 100 =$ _____

d. $1.35 \times 100 =$ _____

e. $5.69 \times 100 =$ _____

f. $7.91 \times 100 =$ _____

❸ Look at the problems and answers in questions 1 and 2. There is a pattern to multiplying by 10 and 100. Then, complete the following table **without** using a calculator.

	Number	× 10	× 100
a.	0.39		
b.	0.71		
c.	0.95		
d.	1.22		
e.	2.53		
f.	5.67		

❹ Use a calculator to divide the following decimals.

a. $0.98 \div 10 =$ _____

b. $0.25 \div 10 =$ _____

c. $0.32 \div 10 =$ _____

d. $1.49 \div 10 =$ _____

e. $8.24 \div 10 =$ _____

f. $6.66 \div 10 =$ _____

❺ Use a calculator to divide the following decimals.

a. $0.69 \div 100 =$ _____

b. $0.34 \div 100 =$ _____

c. $0.09 \div 100 =$ _____

d. $7.88 \div 100 =$ _____

e. $1.21 \div 100 =$ _____

f. $4.72 \div 100 =$ _____

❻ Look at the problems and answers in questions 4 and 5. There is a pattern to dividing by 10 and 100. Then, complete the following table **without** using a calculator.

	Number	÷ 10	÷ 100
a.	0.57		
b.	0.91		
c.	0.04		
d.	3.97		
e.	5.07		
f.	6.23		

Simple Percentages

1 What percentage of each hundreds square is shaded?

a.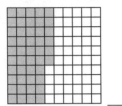

b.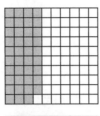

c.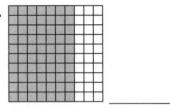

d.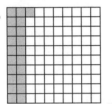

e.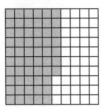

f.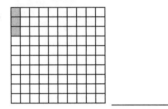

2 For each hundreds square, shade the given percentage.

a. 64%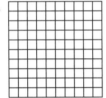

b. 14%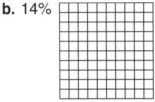

c. 32%

d. 91%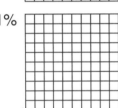

e. 85%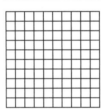

f. 77%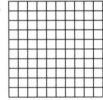

3 Complete the following.

a. 10% means _____ out of 100.

b. 8% means _____ out of 100.

c. 20% means _____ out of 100.

d. _____ means 50 out of 100.

e. _____ means 75 out of 100.

f. _____ means 90 out of 100.

4 Write the percentage that means the following.

a. one-half _____

b. a quarter _____

c. one-tenth _____

d. 80 out of 100 _____

e. 63 out of 100 _____

f. 14 out of 100 _____

5 There were 100 students at the school and 25% were boys. How many students were girls? _____

6 Eighty-four people came to Summer and Tim's wedding. If 100 people were invited, what percentage of people did not come to the wedding? _____

Percentages

1 What percentage of each hundreds square is **not** shaded?

a. 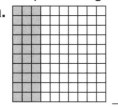 _____   b. 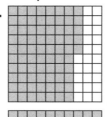 _____   c. 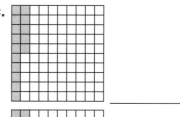 _____

d. 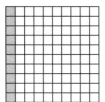 _____   e. 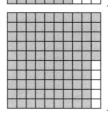 _____   f. 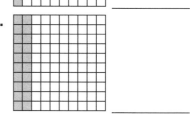 _____

2 Circle the greater amount in each pair.

a. 20%   or   75%   b. 15%   or   10%   c. 100%   or   1%

d. 20%   or   15%   e. 90%   or   9%   f. 18%   or   80%

3 Draw lines to connect the same values.

a. 0.1   35%

b. 0.25   50%

c. 0.35   90%

d. 0.75   10%

e. 0.9   75%

f. 0.5   25%

4 Complete the following table.

	Decimal	Fraction	Percent
a.	0.60	$\frac{}{100}$	%
b.	0.15	$\frac{}{100}$	%
c.	0.	$\frac{35}{100}$	%
d.	0.	$\frac{7}{10}$	%
e.	0.	$\frac{}{100}$	22%
f.	0.	$\frac{}{10}$	80%

5 In a game, Jessie scored:

Level 1: $\frac{26}{100}$ Level 2: $\frac{47}{100}$ Level 3: $\frac{36}{100}$

a. What are each of Jessie's scores as percentages? _____

b. What was Jessie's best-scoring level? _____

6 Bob gave 10% of his 50 marbles to Jackson.
How many marbles did he give? _____

Fractions, Decimals, and Percentages

❶ Write the following fractions as decimals.

a. $\frac{1}{10}$ ——————————

b. $\frac{7}{10}$ ——————————

c. $\frac{1}{4}$ ——————————

d. $\frac{14}{100}$ ——————————

e. $\frac{8}{10}$ ——————————

f. $\frac{36}{100}$ ——————————

❷ Write the following fractions as percentages.

a. $\frac{4}{10}$ ——————————

b. $\frac{3}{10}$ ——————————

c. $\frac{3}{4}$ ——————————

d. $\frac{45}{100}$ ——————————

e. $\frac{2}{10}$ ——————————

f. $\frac{63}{100}$ ——————————

❸ Use <, >, or = to make the following statements true.

a. 0.99 ☐ 99%

b. 60% ☐ $\frac{60}{100}$

c. 50% ☐ $\frac{1}{10}$

d. 0.7 ☐ 77%

e. 5% ☐ 0.5

f. $\frac{3}{4}$ ☐ 75%

❹ Complete the following table.

	Percent	Fraction	Decimal
a.			0.5
b.		$\frac{1}{10}$	
c.			0.25
d.	15%		
e.		$\frac{82}{100}$	
f.	73%		

❺ There are 20 students in a class.

a. If 50% like music, how many students like music? ————————————————

b. If 20% buy their lunch, how many students buy their lunch? ————————————

c. If 25% ride a bike to school, how many students ride a bike to school? ——————

❻ Draw 10 triangles in the box.

a. Shade $\frac{3}{10}$ of the triangles.

b. Circle 50% of the triangles.

c. Draw a smiley face inside 0.2 of the triangles.

Use of Money

1 List the least number of bills and coins needed to make the following amounts. You may use half-dollar coins. Do not use $2 bills.

a. 65¢ _____

b. $2.85 _____

c. $10.25 _____

d. 95¢ _____

e. $4.35 _____

f. $6.75 _____

Use the following items for questions 2 and 3.

art set
$16.75

pencils
$5.75

scissors
$2.15

glue
$1.10

highlighter
$4.39

calculator
$25.95

2 Find the single bill that could be used to cover the cost of the following items.

a. art set _____

b. pencils _____

c. scissors _____

d. glue _____

e. highlighter _____

f. calculator _____

3 If you had $10, would you be able to buy:

a. pencils? _____

b. the glue and scissors? _____

c. 2 highlighters? _____

d. a calculator? _____

e. 2 sets of pencils? _____

f. an art set? _____

4 How many of each bill below makes $100?

a. $50 _____

b. $100 _____

c. $20 _____

d. $5 _____

e. $2 _____

f. $1 _____

5 Morgan bought a smoothie for $3.79.
If she paid with a $5 bill, how much change would she get back? _____

6 Make $20 using any combination of bills or coins in 4 different ways.

a. _____

b. _____

c. _____

d. _____

❶ Add the following amounts.

a. $3.75 +$2.98	**b.** $4.24 +$5.47	**c.** $5.51 +$2.98
d. $1.98 +$6.45	**e.** $1.82 +$3.49	**f.** $6.27 +$2.35

❷ Subtract the following amounts.

a. $6.73 −$2.49	**b.** $9.74 −$3.25	**c.** $8.25 −$4.21
d. $9.50 −$3.67	**e.** $7.54 −$4.99	**f.** $7.11 −$4.53

❸ Find the change from $9.00, if I spent:

a. $5.50. _____   **b.** $6.40. _____   **c.** $7.30. _____

d. $4.55. _____   **e.** $2.90. _____   **f.** $6.25. _____

❹ Find the total of each bill.

a. apples $2.90
 +bananas $1.80

b. apples $2.90
 +oranges $3.60

c. apples $2.90
 +pears $2.50

d. bananas $1.80
 +oranges $3.60

e. apples $2.90
 bananas $1.80
 +pears $2.50

f. bananas $1.80
 pears $2.50
 +oranges $3.60

❺ If Alec bought 2 bags of oranges at $3.60 a bag, how much change would he get back after paying with a $20 bill?

_____

❻ Lisa is saving her money to buy a new bike helmet that costs $25.50. She has $16.36. How much more does Lisa need to save?

_____

Money Multiplication and Division

1 How much money does Mark have in total, if he has:

    a. five 25¢ coins? _____   **b.** three $20 bills? _____

    c. twelve 10¢ coins? _____   **d.** four $5 bills? _____

    e. seven $5 bills? _____   **f.** ten $2 bills? _____

2 How many of each of the following bills or coins are needed to make $20?

    a. 50¢ _____   **b.** $1 _____

    c. $20 _____   **d.** $5 _____

    e. $2 _____   **f.** 10¢ _____

3 Share the following amounts. How much will each person get?

    a. $4 among 2 people _____   **b.** $2 among 4 people _____

    c. $20 among 5 children _____   **d.** $50 among 10 children _____

    e. $100 among 10 teachers _____   **f.** $20 among 8 teachers _____

4 Find the total cost of the following purchases.

    a. 8 apples at 50¢ each _____   **b.** 10 pencils at 30¢ each _____

    c. 6 birthday cards at $2 each _____   **d.** 5 desserts at $3 each _____

    e. 4 bunches of flowers at $10 each _____   **f.** 5 loaves of bread at $3 each _____

5 Mrs. Smith spent the following amounts on each day.

    Monday: $20.75, $30.25, and $10.15

    Thursday: $15.65, $21.50, and $3.90

    a. How much did Mrs. Smith spend each day? _____

    b. What was the difference between her spending on both days? _____

6 Make up a multiplication word problem using the following values: $6 and 4. Then solve it.

_____

_____

_____

Money Rounding and Estimation

① Round each of the following amounts to the nearest 5 cents.

    a. 69¢ _____   **b.** 37¢ _____

    c. 24¢ _____   **d.** 42¢ _____

    e. 19¢ _____   **f.** 83¢ _____

② Round each of the following amounts to the nearest 10 cents.

    a. 79¢ _____   **b.** $0.62 _____

    c. $0.35 _____   **d.** $3.98 _____

    e. $1.44 _____   **f.** $8.71 _____

③ Round each of the following amounts to the nearest whole dollar.

    a. $1.79 _____   **b.** $2.25 _____

    c. $3.46 _____   **d.** $9.95 _____

    e. $0.70 _____   **f.** $4.12 _____

④ Add or subtract each of the following amounts. Then round the answers to the nearest five cents.

a.	**b.**	**c.**	**d.**
$2.95	$3.35	$6.95	$5.15
+$1.73	+$2.58	−$2.47	−$1.91

⑤ Estimate, by first rounding each of the following amounts to the nearest whole dollar.

    a. $4.95 + $6.15 + $2.25 = _____

    b. $11.20 + $2.05 + $5.69 = _____

    c. $19.75 − $8.10 = _____

    d. $8.85 − $3.98 = _____

⑥ A class collected money for charity over five weeks. Estimate how much they collected altogether by rounding each amount to the nearest dollar before adding.

Week 1:	$20.75
Week 2:	$15.95
Week 3:	$17.05
Week 4:	$18.10
Week 5:	$16.90

Symmetry

1 Complete each shape so that it is symmetrical.

a.

b.

c.

d.

e.

f.

2 Which of the following shapes are symmetrical? Write *yes* for those that are and *no* for those that are not.

a. _____

b. _____

c. _____

d. _____

e. _____

f. _____

3 Which of the following letters are symmetrical? Write *yes* for those that are and *no* for those that are not.

a. A _____

b. B _____

c. F _____

d. G _____

e. H _____

f. J _____

4 Which of the following numbers are symmetrical? Write *yes* for those that are and *no* for those that are not.

a. 2 _____

b. 3 _____

c. 4 _____

d. 5 _____

e. 8 _____

f. 0 _____

5 Complete the following table.

	Shape	# of Sides	# of Lines of Symmetry
a.			
b.			
c.			
d.			

6 Draw two different objects that are symmetrical and add in the lines of symmetry.

Shapes

① Identify which of the shapes are 2-dimensional (2D) and which are 3-dimensional (3D).

a. ⬜ _____

b. _____

c. ▽ _____

d. _____

e. _____

f. _____

② Name each of the following shapes. Use the word list in the box to help.

star	octagon	triangle	pentagon	oval	parallelogram

a. △ _____

b. ⬠ _____

c. ◯ _____

d. _____

e. ☆ _____

f. ⯃ _____

③ Color or shade the shapes that are parallelograms.

a. ◇

b. ⏢

c. ▱

d. ▭

e. ⬡

f. ▽

④ Draw each of the following shapes.

a. square

b. circle

c. hexagon

d. rectangle

e. triangle

f. rhombus

⑤ Draw a semicircle (half circle).

⑥ Try your best to draw a regular 10-sided shape (called a decagon).

Plane Shapes

1 Match the name and the shape.

   a. pentagon

   b. parallelogram

   c. hexagon

   d. oval

   e. octagon

   f. rhombus

2 Draw each of the following.

   a. a shape with 4 equal angles and 4 equal sides   **b.** a shape with 1 curve

   c. a shape that has 3 sharp angles   **d.** a shape with 4 equal angles and sets of 2 equal sides

3 Find the number of angles in:

   a. 4 squares. _____   **b.** 3 triangles. _____

   c. 2 pentagons. _____   **d.** 3 octagons. _____

   e. 2 triangles and 3 rectangles. _____   **f.** 5 parallelograms. _____

4 Color or shade the shapes that are trapezoids.

   a.   **b.**   **c.**

   d.   **e.**   **f.**

5 Name a real-life object that comes in the following shapes.

   a. circle _____   **b.** octagon _____

   c. rectangle _____   **d.** triangle _____

6 Write a description for each of the following shapes.

   a. _____

   b. _____

   c. _____

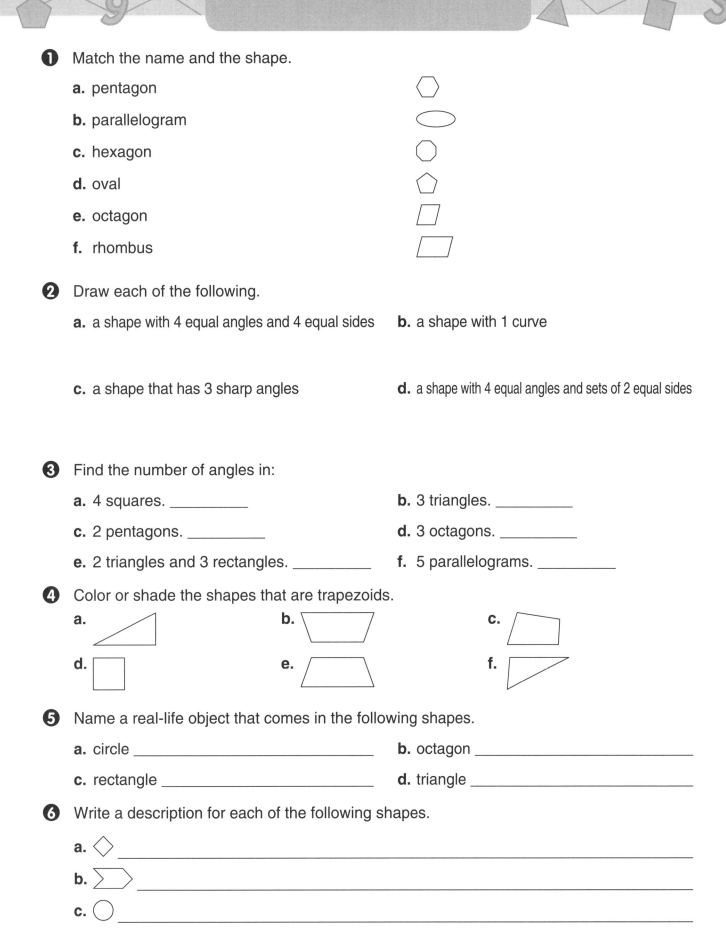

Regular and Irregular Shapes

❶ Color or circle the shapes that are regular. (All side lengths are equal.)

a.

b.

c.

d.

e.

f.

❷ Name the following regular shapes.

a.

b.

c.

_____

_____

_____

d.

e.

f.

_____

_____

_____

❸ Name the following irregular shapes. (Names based on number of sides.)

a.

b.

c.

_____

_____

_____

d.

e.

f.

_____

_____

_____

❹ Draw the following shapes.

a. irregular octagon

b. regular pentagon

c. irregular nonagon

d. square

e. rectangle

f. equilateral triangle

❺ Look around the room. Name two objects that are regular shapes.

_____

❻ Draw a picture using
only irregular shapes.

Angles in Real Life

❶ Do any of the lines in each letter below create a right (90°) angle? Write *yes* or *no*.

a. T _____   **b.** A _____   **c.** Y _____

d. E _____   **e.** L _____   **f.** X _____

❷ Do any of the lines in each letter below create an acute (< 90°) angle? Write *yes* or *no*.

a. V _____   **b.** F _____   **c.** N _____

d. Z _____   **e.** H _____   **f.** M _____

❸ Color the clock faces on which the hands make an angle equal to or less than 90°.

a.   **b.**   **c.**   **d.**   **e.**   **f.**

❹ Draw hands on the clock to show times that represent the following angles.

a. 90°   **b.** 180°

❺ Draw each of the following angles using the starting lines.

a. greater than 45°   **b.** less than 180°   **c.** equal to 90°

d. greater than 180°   **e.** less than 90°   **f.** less than 45°

❻ Draw a picture of a simple house and mark all the different angles in green.

Comparing Angles

Use these angles to answer questions 1–3.

 A B C D

 E F G H I

❶ Are the listed angles less than 90°? Write *yes* or *no*.

a. A _____

b. B _____

c. C _____

d. E _____

e. F _____

f. H _____

❷ Find the larger angle. Circle the correct letter.

a. A or B

b. B or C

c. D or E

d. E or F

e. G or H

f. I or F

❸ Are the listed angles equal to 90°? Write *yes* or *no*.

a. G _____

b. H _____

c. I _____

d. F _____

e. D _____

f. C _____

❹ Order the following angles from the smallest (1) to the largest (6).

a. _____

b. _____

c.  _____

d. _____

e.  _____

f.  _____

❺ Order the following angles from the largest (1) to the smallest (3).

a. _____

b. _____

c. _____

❻ **a.** Draw two angles smaller than:

b. Draw two angles larger than:

Angles — Right, Obtuse, and Acute

1 Are the following angles acute? Write *yes* or *no*.

a.  _____

b. _____

c. _____

d. _____

e. _____

f. _____

2 Using the starting lines, complete each of the following right angles.

a.

b.

c.

d.

e.

f.

3 Are the following angles obtuse? Write *yes* or *no*.

a. _____

b. _____

c. _____

d. _____

e. _____

f. _____

4 Indicate whether each of the following triangles is right-angled or obtuse-angled.

a. _____

b. _____

c. _____

d. _____

e. _____

f. _____

5 Label the following angles as *acute*, *obtuse*, or *right*.

a. _____

b. _____

c. _____

6 Draw an acute-angled triangle (one in which all angles are acute or less than 90°).

Drawing Angles

① Draw an angle that is less than the following.

    a. a right angle   **b.** a straight angle   **c.**

    d.   **e.**   **f.**

② Draw an angle that is greater than the following.

    a. a right angle   **b.** a straight angle   **c.**

    d.   **e.**   **f.**

③ Complete the following right angles.

    a.   **b.**   **c.**

    d.   **e.**   **f.**

④ Label each of the inside angles in the following shapes. Use *a* for acute, *o* for obtuse, and *r* for right.

    a.   **b.**   **c.**

    d.   **e.**    **f.**

⑤ For the following shapes, indicate which of the inside angles are acute (a), obtuse (o), or right (r).

    a.   **b.**    **c.**   **d.**

⑥ Draw a picture that has at least 2 right, 2 obtuse, and 2 acute angles.

Parallel and Perpendicular Lines

1 At how many points does each group of lines cross?

a. _____

b. _____

c.  _____

d. _____

e. _____

f. 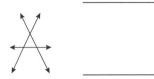 _____

2 Which of the following sets of lines are parallel lines? Write *yes* for those that are and *no* for those that are not.

a.  _____

b. _____

c.  _____

d.  _____

e.  _____

f.  _____

3 Do the following sets of lines have perpendicular lines? Write *yes* or *no*.

a.  _____

b.  _____

c.  _____

d.  _____

e. _____

f. _____

4 Use two different colors to trace the lines on the following shapes to show if and where the parallel lines are.

a.

b.

c.

d.

e.

f.

5 On the following letters, indicate the perpendicular lines with a small square (□) to represent the right angles.

a. E   b. H   c. M   d. T

6 On the following letters, indicate the parallel lines by circling each pair.

a. F   b. A   c. N   d. Z

3D Objects

❶ Name each of the following solids.

a.

_____

b.

_____

c.

_____

d.

_____

e.

_____

f.

_____

❷ A *cross section* is the face that is seen when a 3D object is cut through. For each of the following solids, draw the shape resulting from the cross section beside each one.

a.

b.

c.

d.

e.

f.

❸ Complete the following table.

	Solid	# of Vertices	# of Edges	# of Faces
a.				
b.				
c.				
d.				
e.				
f.				

❹ For the following solids, draw what would be seen if you looked at each from the front, the side, and the top.

Solid	Front	Side	Top
	a.	b.	c.
	d.	e.	f.

❺ Draw a solid shape with:

a. 4 faces.   **b.** 6 faces.   **c.** 8 faces.

❻ What 3D shapes do the following real-life objects best represent?

a. volcano _____

b. wedge of cheese _____

c. marble _____

d. can of soup _____

❶ Copy each of the following.

a.   **b.**   **c.**

d.   **e.**   **f.**

❷ Draw each of the following.

    a. a prism that has 6 rectangular faces   **b.** an object with 2 circles as bases

    c. a pyramid that has a pentagon as a base   **d.** a pyramid that has a 6-sided shape as the base

❸ For the following solids, draw what would be seen if you looked at each from the front, the side, and the top.

Solid	Front	Side	Top
	a.	**b.**	**c.**
	d.	**e.**	**f.**

❹ Draw the different shapes that make up the following objects. You should draw 1 or 2 shapes for each object.

    a.   **b.**   **c.**

    d.   **e.**   **f.**

❺ Draw a real-life object to represent the following shapes.

    a. rectangular prism   **b.** cone

❻ Write a set of instructions for someone drawing a square pyramid.

_____

_____

1 Are these shapes quadrilaterals? Write *yes* or *no*.

a. _____

b. _____

c. _____

d. _____

e. _____

f. _____

2 Draw each of the following.

a. a quadrilateral with 4 equal sides and 4 right angles

b. a triangle with 3 equal sides

c. a quadrilateral that has only 1 set of parallel sides

d. a triangle with 3 sides of different lengths

e. a quadrilateral that has 4 equal sides and the opposite angles are equal

f. a triangle with 2 equal sides

3 State the number of angles inside each of the following shapes.

a. _____

b. _____

c. _____

d. _____

e. _____

f. _____

4 Do these shapes have parallel sides? Write *yes* or *no*.

a. _____

b. _____

c. _____

d. _____

e. _____

f. _____

5 Draw 4 different quadrilaterals.

6 Draw 4 different triangles.

Polygons

❶ Name each of the polygons.

a. _____

b. _____

c. _____

d. _____

e. _____

f. _____

❷ State the number of sides for each of the following polygons.

a. pentagon _____

b. hexagon _____

c. triangle _____

d. square _____

e. octagon _____

f. parallelogram _____

❸ State the number of diagonals for each of the following polygons.

a. triangle _____

b. trapezoid _____

c. pentagon _____

d. rectangle _____

e. hexagon _____

f. octagon _____

❹ Draw in all the lines of symmetry for each of the polygons.

a.

b.

c.

d.

e.

f.

❺ What is the name for a 9-sided polygon? _____

❻ Try your best to draw a regular 9-sided shape.

Prisms

❶ Are the following objects prisms? Write *yes* or *no*.

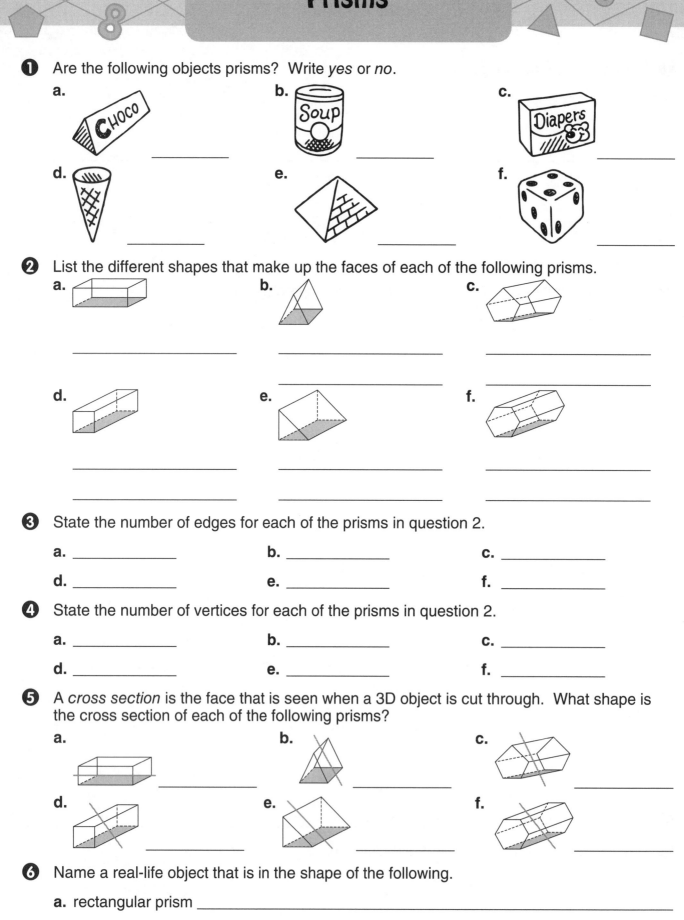

a. _____

b. _____

c. _____

d. _____

e. _____

f. _____

❷ List the different shapes that make up the faces of each of the following prisms.

a. _____

b. _____

c. _____

d. _____
_____

e. _____
_____

f. _____
_____

❸ State the number of edges for each of the prisms in question 2.

a. _____

b. _____

c. _____

d. _____

e. _____

f. _____

❹ State the number of vertices for each of the prisms in question 2.

a. _____

b. _____

c. _____

d. _____

e. _____

f. _____

❺ A *cross section* is the face that is seen when a 3D object is cut through. What shape is the cross section of each of the following prisms?

a. _____

b. _____

c. _____

d. _____

e. _____

f. _____

❻ Name a real-life object that is in the shape of the following.

a. rectangular prism _____

b. triangular prism _____

Cylinders, Cones, and Spheres

1 Are these solids cylinders? Write *yes* or *no*.

a. _____

b. _____

c. Soup _____

d. _____

e. _____

f. _____

2 Write the name of each solid under its picture.

a. _____

b. _____

c. _____

d. _____

e. _____

f. _____

3 State the number of curved surfaces in each of the following solids.

a. cone _____

b. sphere _____

c. cylinder _____

d. square pyramid _____

e. cube _____

f. rectangular prism _____

4 State the number of edges in each of the following solids.

a. cone _____

b. cylinder _____

c. rectangular prism _____

d. sphere _____

e. cube _____

f. triangular prism _____

5 State the number of flat faces in each of the solids in question 4.

a. _____

b. _____

c. _____

d. _____

e. _____

f. _____

6 A *cross section* is the face that is seen when a 3D object is cut through. For each of the following solids, draw the shape resulting from the cross section beside each one.

a.

b.

c.

Pyramids

1 Which of these solids are pyramids? Write *yes* or *no*.

a. _____

b. _____

c. _____

d. _____

e. _____

f.  _____

2 State the number of vertices (v) and edges (e) for each of the following pyramids.

a.

v = _____ e = _____

b.

v = _____ e = _____

c.

v = _____ e = _____

d.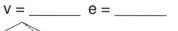

v = _____ e = _____

e.

v = _____ e = _____

f.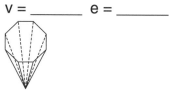

v = _____ e = _____

3 Draw the shape or shapes that make up the different faces for each of the pyramids in question 2. You should draw 1 or 2 shapes for each pyramid.

a.

b.

c.

d.

e.

f.

4 Name the shape of each base.

a. _____

b. _____

c. _____

d. _____

e. _____

f. _____

5 Name each of the pyramids in question 4.

a. _____

b. _____

c. _____

d. _____

e. _____

f. _____

6 A *cross section* is the face that is seen when a 3D object is cut through. What shape is the cross section of each of the following pyramids?

a. _____

b. _____

Nets and 3D Objects

1 Match the object and its net.

a.
b.
c.
d.
e.
f.

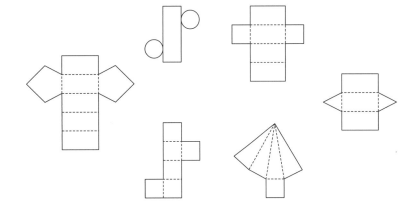

2 Would the following nets fold to make a closed 3D shape? Write *yes* or *no*.

a.  _____

b. _____

c.  _____

d.  _____

e. _____

f. _____

3 Name the 3D object each net will make when it is folded.

a.

b.

c.

_____ _____ _____

d.

e.

f.

_____ _____ _____

4 A *cross section* is the face that is seen when a 3D object is cut through. For each of the following solids, draw the shape resulting from the cross section beside each one.

a.
b.
c.
d.

5 What 3D shape can be made using the following shapes as faces?

 _____

6 Draw the net of the cereal box.

Movement of Shapes

1 Reflect each of the following shapes by drawing the mirror image on the other side of the line.

a.   **b.**   **c.**

d.   **e.**   **f.**

2 Translate each of the following shapes by "moving" them to the right.

a.   **b.**   **c.**

d.   **e.**   **f.**

3 Rotate each of the following shapes by drawing what the shape would look like after being turned clockwise about one point from the center.

a.   **b.**   **c.**

d.   **e.**   **f.**

4 Use the words *reflect*, *translate*, or *rotate* to describe the movement of the following shapes.

a.    **b.**   **c.**

_____   _____   _____

d.   **e.**   **f.**

_____   _____   _____

5 Continue the pattern by reflection.

6 Rotate the book across the table.

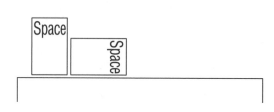

Tessellation

1 A **tessellation** is a pattern of one or more identical shapes that fit together without any gaps or overlaps. Do these shapes tessellate? Write *yes* or *no*.

a. _____

b. _____

c. _____

d. _____

e. _____

f. _____

2 Do these shapes tessellate? Write *yes* or *no*.

a. _____

b. _____

c. _____

d. _____

e. _____

f. _____

3 Continue the following tessellations.

a.

b.

c.

d.

4 Create tessellations using the following shapes.

a.

b.

c.

d.

5 Draw a shape that will not tessellate.

6 Create your own tessellation pattern.

Position — Giving Directions

1 Which animal is:

   a. left of the tiger? _____

   b. left of the hippo? _____

   c. right of the tiger? _____

   d. right of the lion? _____

   e. left of the elephant? _____

   f. right of the horse? _____

2 Here is a set of drawers filled with school supplies. Which item is found at the following positions?

   a. top left corner _____

   b. far right of middle shelf _____

   c. top right corner _____

   d. in the center _____

   e. middle of top shelf _____

   f. left of the pens _____

glue	paper clips	markers
tape	rubber bands	pencils
labels	staples	pens

3 Color the square in the:

   a. top row, far left, green.

   b. top row, second from the left, red.

   c. bottom row, second from the right, blue.

   d. Draw a triangle in the middle row, 4 from the right.

   e. Draw a circle in the bottom row, 4 from the left.

   f. What position is the star? _____

4 For the food items on the table, describe the position of:

   a. the bread. _____

   b. the strawberry. _____

   c. the pineapple. _____

   d. the cheese. _____

   e. the cake. _____

   f. the drink. _____

5 **a.** Which animal is left of the bear in question 1? _____

   b. In question 2, which item is in the second row, third from the left? _____

   c. On the grid in question 3, draw a square in the center row, 4th from the left.

   d. For the food items in question 4, describe the position of the carrot. _____

6 Complete the maze to find the prize. Write the path you took using directional words.

_____

Start ⟶

Compass Directions

1 Complete the compass rose using:
E, S, W, NE, NW, SE.

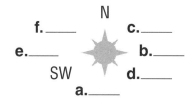

N

f.____   c.____

e.____   b.____

SW   d.____

a.____

2 Tom is standing at X. What can he see if he looks:

a. south? _____

b. west? _____

c. north? _____

d. southwest? _____

e. northeast? _____

f. northwest? _____

tree

house   school

mountains — X — road

park   beach

boat

3 Using the diagram from question 2, what direction does Tom need to look to see:

a. the road? _____   **b.** the beach? _____

c. the tree? _____   **d.** the mountains? _____

e. the school? _____   **f.** the house? _____

4 From the X, draw:

a. a star to the north.

b. a moon to the south.

c. a sun to the east.

d. a cloud to the northwest.

e. a rainbow to the southeast.

f. a lightning bolt to the west.

X

5 From the heart, draw a diamond to the southwest.

♥

6 To see Sally, which way does the:

a. worm look? _____

b. cat look? _____

c. dog look? _____

bird

bee

Sally

cat   dog

worm

Coordinates

1 What shapes are found at the following coordinates?

a. (B, 3) _____ **b.** (C, 1) _____

c. (D, 1) _____ **d.** (C, 2) _____

e. (D, 3) _____ **f.** (B, 1) _____

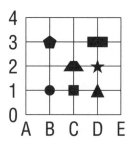

2 Draw the given shape at each point on the grid.

a. (B, 1) ★ **b.** (C, 4) ◆

c. (C, 0) ■ **d.** (E, 4) ●

e. (D, 2) ▲ **f.** (B, 3) ☾

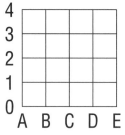

3 For the large letter **E** shown on the grid, give the coordinates for each labeled point.

a. _____

b. _____

c. _____

d. _____

e. _____

f. _____

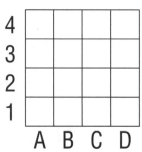

4 On the grid, draw:

a. a square in (B, 3). **b.** a circle in (C, 4).

c. a diamond in (A, 2). **d.** a rectangle in (D, 1).

e. an octagon in (C, 2). **f.** an oval in (A, 1).

5 Give the coordinates of the star from the grid in question 1. _____

6 In the box to the right, create a grid and write the coordinates for your initials. Give them to a partner to solve.

Grids

1 Write the coordinates of the following creatures.

    a. cat _____   **b.** spider _____

    c. ladybug _____   **d.** chick _____

    e. ant _____   **f.** penguin _____

2 Using the grid above, name the creatures found at the following coordinates.

    a. (A, 5) _____   **b.** (D, 2) _____

    c. (C, 3) _____   **d.** (B, 2) _____

    e. (D, 4) _____   **f.** (C, 5) _____

3 What are the coordinates of the following symbols?

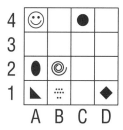

    a. ◎ _____   **b.** ◆ _____

    c. ● _____   **d.** ◣ _____

    e. ⸬ _____   **f.** ⬮ _____

4 In the grid of question 3, draw:

    a. a rectangle in (D, 3).   **b.** stripes in (C,1).   **c.** a $ in (B, 4).

    d. a square in (B, 3).   **e.** a dot in (C, 2).   **f.** a star in (D, 2).

5 **a.** What are the coordinates of the pig in the grid of question 1? _____

    b. What animal is found in (A, 4) in the grid of question 1? _____

    c. What are the coordinates of the happy face in the grid of question 3? _____

    d. Draw half a circle on the grid of question 3 in (D, 4). _____

6 After completing questions 4 and 5, name all the blank spaces from the grids in questions 1 and 3.

    Question 1: _____

    Question 3: _____

Puzzles

1 A magic square is where numbers are arranged in a square so that they add up to the same total vertically, horizontally, and diagonally. Complete each magic square for the total given.

a. 15:

8		6
		7
	9	

b. 18:

3		
5	9	

c. 21:

6		
	7	
10		

d. 27:

15		
		13
7	17	

e. 69:

11		24
22	35	

f. 177:

	89	
		113
101	29	

2 Using the tangram as a guide, draw in the lines showing the shapes that are used to make up the following images.

a.   **b.**   **c.**   **d.**

3 Work backwards to find the original number, if I started with that number and:

a. × 2, then + 5 and the solution was 15. _____

b. − 3, then × 2 and the solution was 12. _____

c. ÷ 3, then − 8 and the solution was 1. _____

d. + 10, then − 5 and the solution was 25. _____

4 Describe each of the following as a *reflection*, *translation*, or *rotation*.

a.   **b.**   **c.**

_____   _____   _____

d.   **e.**   **f.**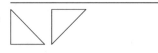

_____   _____   _____

5 Use the clues to find the mystery number. I'm thinking of a four-digit number in which:

- you can get the fourth digit by adding together two of the others.
- the third digit is twice the first.
- the product of the first and second digits is twenty.
- the second digit is larger than the first.

			9

= Mystery Number

6 Design your own magic square that has the magic number 30. Give four numbers and leave the rest blank for a friend to solve.

Paper Folding and Shapes

1 Can these shapes be obtained by evenly folding a square piece of paper? Write *yes* or *no*.

a. ◺ _____

b. ⬡ _____

c. ▭ _____

d. ◯ _____

e. △ _____

f. □ _____

2 For the tangram, name each of the labeled shapes.

f (whole shape)

a. _____

b. _____

c. _____

d. _____

e. _____

f. _____

3 For the tangram, name each of the labeled shapes.

a. _____

b. _____

c. _____

d. _____

e. _____

f. _____

4 Can each shape be evenly folded to make the new shape? Answer *true* or *false*.

a. ▭ can be folded to ◹ _____

b. □ can be folded to ◺ _____

c. △ can be folded to □ _____

d. ▭ can be folded to ▭ _____

e. △ can be folded to △ _____

f. ▱ can be folded to ◿ _____

5 Draw six lines on this shape to make 12 triangles.

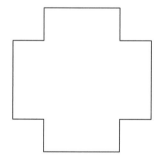

6 Complete the simple paper-folding exercise using a piece of square paper.

    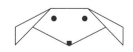

1 Write the time that is **one minute after** the following times.

a. 5 min. past 8:00 _____

b. 10 min. to 9:00 _____

c. 15 min. past 6:00 _____

d. 25 min. to 7:00 _____

e. 10 min. past 2:00 _____

f. 5 min. to 10:00 _____

2 How many minutes does it take for the minute hand to:

a. move from the 4 to the 5? _____

b. move from the 7 to the 9? _____

c. move from the 1 to the 4? _____

d. move from the 12 to the 6? _____

e. move from the 12 to the 8? _____

f. move from the 12 to the 11? _____

3 Complete the label for each time shown.

a.   **b.**   **c.**   **d.**   **e.**   **f.**

_____ to _____   _____ to _____   _____ to _____   _____ past _____   _____ past _____   _____ past _____

4 Complete each clock to show the time given.

a. 5 min. to 7   **b.** 20 min. past 3   **c.** quarter to 9   **d.** quarter past 6   **e.** half past 3   **f.** half past 8

5 Write the time shown on each clock in two different ways.

a.   **b.**   **c.**   **d.**   **e.**

_____   _____   _____   _____   _____

_____   _____   _____   _____   _____

6 Draw a clock face to show 3:15.

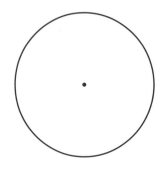

Digital and Analog Time

1 Use < or > to make the statements true.

a. 5 days ☐ 1 week

b. 20 hours ☐ 1 day

c. 65 seconds ☐ 1 minute

d. 19 days ☐ 2 weeks

e. 25 days ☐ 1 month

f. 70 minutes ☐ 1 hour

2 Complete the label for each time shown.

a. `4:17`   **b.** `6:49`   **c.** `8:29`   **d.** `10:56`   **e.** `7:35`   **f.** `1:35`

_____ past _____   _____ to _____   _____ past _____   _____ to _____   _____ past _____   _____ to _____

3 On each clock face, show the time given.

a. 12:17   **b.** 3:57   **c.** 6:26   **d.** 2:51   **e.** 8:06   **f.** 10:46

4 How many minutes will it take for the time to reach the next hour?

a. `6:43`   **b.** `4:44`   **c.** `7:06`   **d.** `4:57`   **e.** `1:35`   **f.** `1:56`

_____ _____ _____ _____ _____ _____

5 On each clock face, draw the time given, and then write it in digital form below.

a. quarter past 7   **b.** half past 2   **c.** quarter to 8   **d.** quarter past 11   **e.** quarter to 1   **f.** half past 8

 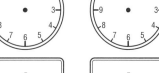 

6 If school starts at 8:45 a.m. and finishes at 3:15 p.m., how long is the school day? _____

Calendars

❶ Complete the following.

    a. 60 minutes = _____ hour   **b.** _____ seconds = 2 minutes

    c. 1 year = _____ months   **d.** 2 weeks = _____ days

    e. _____ hours = 1 day   **f.** _____ hours = 180 minutes

❷ Name the month that comes before:

    a. June. _____   **b.** September. _____

    c. October. _____   **d.** December. _____

    e. April. _____   **f.** February. _____

❸ What does each of the following abbreviations stand for?

    a. Feb. _____   **b.** Mon. _____

    c. Wed. _____   **d.** Dec. _____

    e. Jan. _____   **f.** Sep. _____

❹ Look at this calendar. What day is:

    a. March 19th? _____

    b. March 25th? _____

    c. March 7th? _____

    d. March 30th? _____

    e. the first day of the month? _____

    f. the last day of the month? _____

MARCH						
Su	**M**	**Tu**	**W**	**Th**	**F**	**Sa**
			1	2	3	4
5	6	7	8	9	10	11
12	13	14	15	16	17	18
19	20	21	22	23	24	25
26	27	28	29	30	31	

❺ Calculate the number of days from:

    a. March 4th to 10th. _____   **b.** March 17th to 29th. _____

    c. March 1st to 15th. _____   **d.** March 6th to 21st. _____

    e. March 1st to 21st. _____   **f.** March 27th to 30th. _____

❻ Using the calendar in question 4, write the date for the following days in March.

    a. the first Wednesday _____   **b.** the last Sunday _____

    c. the first Monday _____   **d.** the last Friday _____

    e. the second Tuesday _____   **f.** the fourth Thursday _____

Time Lines and Timetables

1 Lin's morning is shown on the time line. What time did Lin:

    a. have breakfast? _____

    b. start recess? _____

    c. leave for school? _____

    d. have music class? _____

    e. wake up? _____

    f. start school? _____

```
6:30 ┼ Woke up
7:00 ┼ Took a shower
7:30 ┼ Had breakfast
8:00 ┼ Fed dog
8:30 ┼ Left for school
9:00 ┼ Started school
9:30 ┼ Music class
10:00 ┼
10:30 ┼
11:00 ┼ Started recess
```

2 Label the time line using letters a.–f. to match the events during a year in Tommy's life.

    a. Started school in February

    b. Turned 5 in July

    c. Got a pet dog in April

    d. Went on vacation in June

    e. Joined the soccer team in May

    f. Has school project in March

February | March | April | May | June | July

3 At what time does the bus arrive at the following locations?

    a. Running Lane _____

    b. Cricket Road _____

    c. Football Street _____

    d. Swimming Hole _____

    e. Ballet Bend _____

    f. Hockey Street _____

BUS TIMETABLE	
Location	**Arriving Time**
Hockey St.	7:10
Swimming Hole	7:20
Running Ln.	7:40
Cricket Rd.	7:55
Ballet Bend	8:15
Basketball Rd.	8:25
Football St.	8:40

4 Using the timetable in question 3, at which location does the bus arrive at:

    a. 7:20? _____   **b.** 8:40? _____

    c. 8:25? _____   **d.** 5 minutes to 8? _____

    e. quarter past 8? _____   **f.** 10 minutes past 7? _____

5 **a.** Using the time line in question 1, at what time did
      Lin feed her dog? _____

    b. At what time does the bus arrive at Basketball
       Road on the timetable in question 3? _____

    c. At which location does the bus arrive at 20 minutes
       to 8 on the timetable in question 3? _____

6 If the bus in question 3 is 30 minutes late, give the time it arrives at:

    a. Hockey Street. _____   **b.** Cricket Road. _____

Length

❶ Complete the following.

    a. _____ inches = 1 foot   **b.** _____ feet = 1 yard   **c.** _____ inches = 1 yard

    d. True or false? 1 cm is shorter than 1 in. _____

❷ Estimate as labeled (in centimeters or inches) and then measure the length of each line. (E = estimate, A = actual length)

    a. E: _____ cm, A = _____ cm

    b. E: _____ cm, A = _____ cm

    c. E: _____ in., A = _____ in.

    d. E: _____ in., A = _____ in.

    e. E: _____ in., A = _____ in.

    f. E: _____ in., A = _____ in.

❸ Draw lines to the correct lengths as given below.

    a. 4 in.

    b. 3 in.

    c. 2 cm

    d. 6 cm

❹ State the measurement—cm, in., or ft.—that would best be used to measure the length of the following.

    a. pencil _____   **b.** car _____

    c. paper clip _____   **d.** book _____

    e. basketball court _____   **f.** toothpick _____

❺ List five objects that are less than 2 inches long.

_____

_____

❻ Measure the length of your pencil to the nearest inch. _____

Length with Decimals

① Write the following lengths in decimal form.

    a. $9\frac{1}{2}$ cm = _____ cm

    b. $6\frac{1}{4}$ in. = _____ in.

    c. $2\frac{3}{4}$ in. = _____ in.

    d. 10 ft. 6 in. = _____ ft.

② Complete the following statements with < or > to make them true.

    a. 15 cm ☐ 20 cm   **b.** 1.5 cm ☐ 1.2 cm   **c.** 11 in. ☐ 9 in.

    d. 14 in. ☐ 1 ft.   **e.** 4.5 in. ☐ 1 ft.   **f.** 4 ft. ☐ 1 yd.

③ Measure the length of each line as labeled (centimeters or inches). Record the lengths in decimal form.

    a. _____ cm

    b. _____ in.

    c. _____ in.

    d. _____ cm

    e. _____ in.

    f. _____ in.

④ Draw lines to the correct lengths as given below.

    a. 4.25 in.

    b. 5.5 cm

    c. 2.5 in.

    d. 3.75 in.

⑤ Six competitors entered the long jump competition. Their jumps were measured in meters. Order their jumps from longest (1) to shortest (6).

    a. Cooper   4.68 m _____   **b.** Andy   5.79 m _____

    c. Roger   7.26 m _____   **d.** Scott   6.75 m _____

    e. Henry   5.32 m _____   **f.** Jerry   6.98 m _____

⑥ Ralph's dad used the below lengths of wire for a project. How much total wire did he use?

    3.7 ft., 8.6 ft., 5.2 ft., and 7.9 ft.   Total = _____

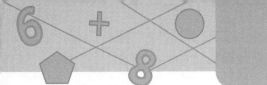
Perimeter

1 Perimeter is the distance around the outside of a shape. Find the perimeter of each of the following shapes.

a. $P =$ ____ + ____ + ____ + ____ = ____ in.

a.

b. $P =$ ____ + ____ + ____ = ____ in.

b.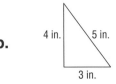

c. $P =$ ____ + ____ + ____ + ____ + ____ + ____ = ____ ft.

c.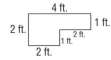

d. $P =$ ____ + ____ + ____ + ____ = ____ ft.

d.

2 A short line drawn through the sides of shapes means that those side lengths are the same. Find the perimeter of each of the following shapes.

a.

b.

c.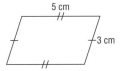

d.

$P =$ _____ $P =$ _____ $P =$ _____ $P =$ _____

3 Find the perimeter of the following rectangles.

a. L = 8 cm   W = 5 cm   P = _____   **b.** L = 10 in. W = 9 in.   P = _____

c. L = 25 ft.   W = 10 ft.   P = _____   **d.** L = 31 ft.   W = 7 ft.   P = _____

4 Find the perimeter of the following regular shapes.

a. square, side length = 7 in.   P = _____   **b.** triangle, side length = 5 in.   P = _____

c. pentagon, side length = 2 ft. P = _____   **d.** hexagon, side length = 6 in.   P = _____

5 Find the perimeter of the following shape.

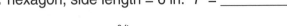
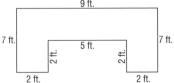

$P =$ _____

6 Draw a square that has a perimeter of:

a. 12 cm.   **b.** 20 cm.

Area

1 Area is the size of a surface. It is measured in square units. Find the area of each of the following shapes by counting the squares. Each square equals 1 square unit (unit²).

a.

$A =$ _____ units²

b.

$A =$ _____ units²

c.

$A =$ _____ units²

d.

$A =$ _____ units²

e.

$A =$ _____ units²

f.

$A =$ _____ units²

2 Find the shaded area of each shape by counting the shaded squares. Remember, two half-shaded squares count as one shaded square.

a.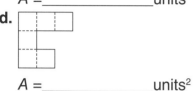

$A =$ _____ units²

b.

$A =$ _____ units²

c.

$A =$ _____ units²

d.

$A =$ _____ units²

3 Name the unit of measurement—in.² or ft.²—that would be best used to find the area of the following.

a. a parking lot _____   b. a slice of bread _____   c. a rug _____

d. a kitchen floor _____   e. a playground _____   f. a playing card _____

4 In squares and rectangles, area can also be found by multiplying the length by the width ($A = L \times W$). Find the area of the following shapes.

a.
4 cm
3 cm

$A =$ _____

b.
5 ft.

$A =$ _____

c.
9 in.
6 in.

$A =$ _____

d.
7 in.

$A =$ _____

5 Find the area of rectangles with the following side lengths.

	Length (in.)	Width (in.)	Area (in.²)
a.	10	4	
b.	12	9	
c.	11	8	
d.	7	3	

6 Find the area of the following triangles. First find the area as if the shape was a rectangle, then divide the area in half to find the area of the triangle, $A = (L \times W) \div 2$.

a.
5 cm
4 cm

$A =$ _____

b.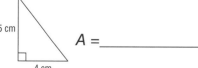
10 in.
6 in.

$A =$ _____

Area and Perimeter

❶ Write each of the following in the short form.

    a. 15 square centimeters _____   **b.** 49 square meters _____

    c. 87 square inches _____   **d.** 35 square feet _____

    e. 74 square yards _____

❷ Complete with < or > to make the number statements true.

    a. 45 in.² ☐ 45 cm²   **b.** 60 cm² ☐ 60 ft.²

    c. 90 cm² ☐ 90 m²   **d.** 26 ft.² ☐ 26 yd.²

❸ Find the area (in units²) of each of the following. Each square equals 1 square unit.

    a. _____   **b.** _____   **c.** _____

    d. _____   **e.** _____   **f.** _____

❹ Find the perimeter (in units) of each of the following. Each square has side lengths of 1 unit.

    a. _____   **b.** _____   **c.** _____

    d. _____   **e.** _____   **f.** _____

❺ Draw a shape with a perimeter of 16 cm.

❻ Draw a shape with an area of 8 cm².

Weight in Ounces and Pounds

1 Record the weight shown on each scale in pounds (lb.).

a.

_____ lb.

b.

_____ lb.

c.

_____ lb.

d.

_____ lb.

e.

_____ lb.

f.

_____ lb.

2 There are 16 ounces (oz.) in 1 pound. Order the following food items from heaviest (1) to lightest (6).

a.

4 lb. _____

b.

1 lb. _____

c.

14 oz. _____

d.

6.5 oz. _____

e.

4.5 oz. _____

f.

8 oz. _____

3 Would ounces (oz.) or pounds (lb.) be better used to weigh the following?

a. a child _____

b. a computer _____

c. 2 mushrooms _____

d. an elephant _____

e. a slice of bread _____

f. an apple _____

4 How many ounces are there in the following weights? Remember, 16 ounces = 1 pound.

a. $\frac{1}{2}$ lb. _____

b. $\frac{3}{4}$ lb. _____

c. $\frac{1}{4}$ lb. _____

d. $1\frac{1}{2}$ lb. _____

5 How many grapefruits are needed to weigh 1 lb., if each grapefruit weighs 8 oz.? _____

6 How many more ounces must be added to each of the following to make $1\frac{1}{2}$ pounds?

a. 13 oz. _____

b. 1 lb. _____

Arrangements

1 Are the shapes below a possible arrangement of the shapes in the box? Write *yes* or *no*.

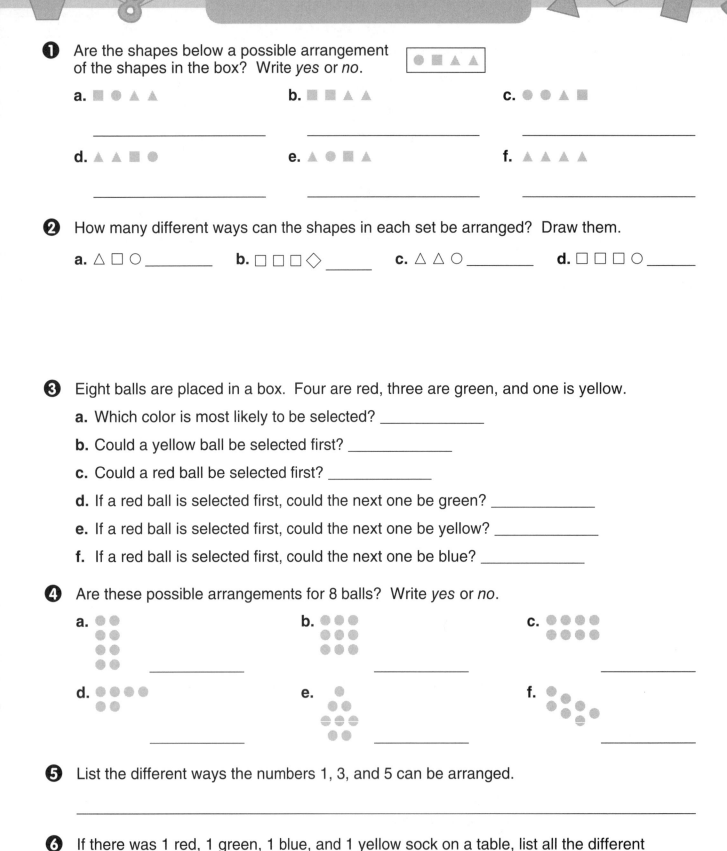

a. ■ ● ▲ ▲

b. ■ ■ ▲ ▲

c. ● ● ▲ ■

d. ▲ ▲ ■ ●

e. ▲ ● ■ ▲

f. ▲ ▲ ▲ ▲

2 How many different ways can the shapes in each set be arranged? Draw them.

a. △ □ ○ _____

b. □ □ □ ◇ _____

c. △ △ ○ _____

d. □ □ □ ○ _____

3 Eight balls are placed in a box. Four are red, three are green, and one is yellow.

a. Which color is most likely to be selected? _____

b. Could a yellow ball be selected first? _____

c. Could a red ball be selected first? _____

d. If a red ball is selected first, could the next one be green? _____

e. If a red ball is selected first, could the next one be yellow? _____

f. If a red ball is selected first, could the next one be blue? _____

4 Are these possible arrangements for 8 balls? Write *yes* or *no*.

a. _____

b. _____

c. _____

d. _____

e. _____

f. _____

5 List the different ways the numbers 1, 3, and 5 can be arranged.

_____

6 If there was 1 red, 1 green, 1 blue, and 1 yellow sock on a table, list all the different possible combinations of pairs of socks. Use R, G, B, and Y in your list to represent the different socks.

_____

Probability

1 In the bag, there are 4 green candies, 2 red candies, 1 blue candy, 7 yellow candies, 3 pink candies, and 4 orange candies.

  a. Which color is most likely to be selected? _____

  b. Which color is least likely to be selected? _____

  c. Is red more likely to be selected than blue? _____

  d. Is pink more likely to be selected than yellow? _____

  e. Is orange less likely to be selected than green? _____

  f. Which 2 colors have equal chance of selection? _____

2 In a hat, there are 2 red and 2 green marbles. If Mia selects 1 marble, what is the probability she will:

  a. select a colored marble? _____   **b.** select a red marble? _____

  c. select a blue marble? _____   **d.** select a green marble? _____

  e. not select a red marble? _____   **f.** not select a green marble? _____

3 Using the words *impossible, unlikely, equal chance, likely,* and *certain,* describe the chance of landing on the shaded regions of the following spinners.

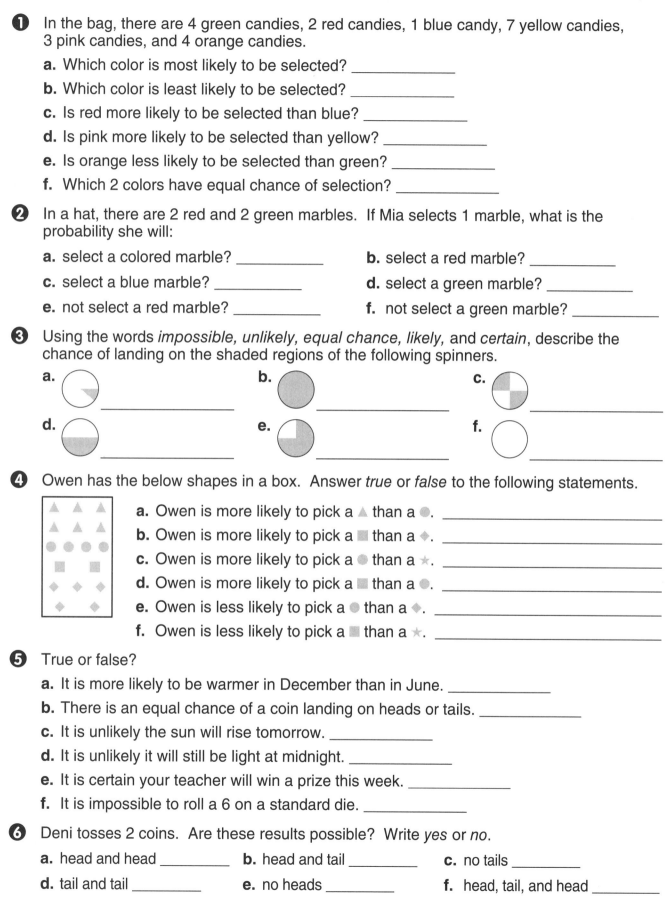

  a. _____   **b.** _____   **c.** _____

  d. _____   **e.** _____   **f.** _____

4 Owen has the below shapes in a box. Answer *true* or *false* to the following statements.

  a. Owen is more likely to pick a ▲ than a ●. _____

  b. Owen is more likely to pick a ■ than a ◆. _____

  c. Owen is more likely to pick a ● than a ★. _____

  d. Owen is more likely to pick a ■ than a ●. _____

  e. Owen is less likely to pick a ● than a ◆. _____

  f. Owen is less likely to pick a ■ than a ★. _____

5 True or false?

  a. It is more likely to be warmer in December than in June. _____

  b. There is an equal chance of a coin landing on heads or tails. _____

  c. It is unlikely the sun will rise tomorrow. _____

  d. It is unlikely it will still be light at midnight. _____

  e. It is certain your teacher will win a prize this week. _____

  f. It is impossible to roll a 6 on a standard die. _____

6 Deni tosses 2 coins. Are these results possible? Write *yes* or *no*.

  a. head and head _____   **b.** head and tail _____   **c.** no tails _____

  d. tail and tail _____   **e.** no heads _____   **f.** head, tail, and head _____

Picture Graphs

1 The following graph shows data about the color of houses. Find how many houses are:

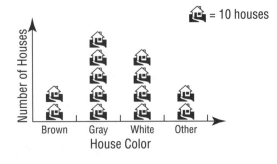

   a. gray. _____

   b. brown. _____

   c. white. _____

   d. other colors. _____

   e. represented on the graph. _____

   f. What does 🏠 represent? _____

2 Give the times during which the number of computers used was:

   a. 25. _____

   b. 20. _____

   c. 10. _____

   d. 15. _____

   e. more than 15. _____

   f. less than 15. _____

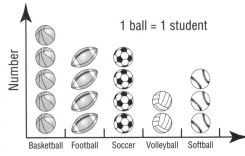

Times	Computers Used
9:00–10:00	🖥️ 🖥️
10:00–11:00	🖥️ 🖥️ 🖥️
11:00–12:00	🖥️ 🖥️ 🖥️ 🖥️
12:00–1:00	🖥️ 🖥️ 🖥️
1:00–2:00	🖥️ 🖥️ 🖥️ 🖥️ 🖥️

🖥️ = 5 computers

3 In a class, the number of students playing each sport is shown in the graph.

   a. What was the most popular sport? _____

   b. What was the least popular sport? _____

   c. Which sports had equal popularity? _____

   d. How many students played football _____

   e. Which sport had 3 students playing? _____

   f. Was football more popular than softball? _____

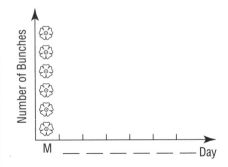

4 Talia kept a total of the number of bunches of flowers sold each day. From the data, complete the picture graph, where ✿ = 1 bunch.

Day	Number
M	6
T	4
W	5
Th	3
F	2
S	7
Su	3

5 **a.** What was the most popular color of house in question 1? _____

   b. What was the total number of computers used between 9:00 and 12:00 in question 2? _____

   c. What was the total number of students playing soccer and basketball in question 3? _____

   d. What was the total number of bunches of flowers sold in question 4? _____

6 On a separate sheet of paper, draw a picture graph of the number of boys and the number of girls in your class. Don't forget to include yourself!

Tally Marks and Tables

1 Emily tossed a coin and kept a tally of the results. How many times did she:

Heads	ʜʜ ʜʜ ʜʜ ‖‖‖
Tails	ʜʜ ʜʜ ʜʜ ʜʜ ‖

a. toss the coin? _____

b. get heads? _____

c. get tails? _____

What fraction of the time did she:

d. get heads? _____

e. get tails? _____

f. not get heads? _____

2 Complete the tally table on the right about favorite sports.

	Sport	Tally	Total
a.	tennis		5
b.	swimming		1
c.	football		8
d.	baseball		7
e.	basketball		5
f.	other		4

3 Answer the following questions using the data from question 2.

a. How many people were surveyed altogether? _____

b. What was the most popular sport? _____

c. What was the least popular sport? _____

d. Which sports had equal popularity? _____

e. How many more people chose baseball than basketball? _____

f. Altogether, how many chose tennis and baseball? _____

4 Below is a tally table about students' favorite drinks.

Drinks	Boys	Girls
milk	‖	ʜʜ
water	ʜʜ	‖‖‖
juice	‖	‖
other	‖	‖

a. What was the most popular drink for boys? _____

b. What was the most popular drink for girls? _____

c. How many girls preferred water? _____

d. How many boys preferred milk? _____

e. What was the most popular drink? _____

f. What was the least popular drink? _____

5 Complete the tally table using the information from the graph.

	Group	Tally	Number
a.	A	ʜʜ ‖‖‖	
b.	B	ʜʜ ʜʜ ʜʜ	
c.	C		
d.	D		
e.	E		6
f.	F		9

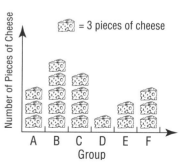

= 3 pieces of cheese

6 On a separate sheet of paper, create your own tally table about the hair color of all the students in your class. Don't forget to include yourself!

Reading Graphs and Tables

1 Use the graph to answer the following questions.
How many cars were parked in the lot on:

a. Tuesday? _____

b. Thursday? _____

c. Thursday and Friday? _____

What day(s) was the parking lot:

d. most full? _____

e. least full? _____

f. How many more cars on
Monday than Thursday? _____

Day	Number of Cars in Parking Lot
Mon.	🚗🚗🚗🚗🚗🚗🚗🚗
Tue.	🚗🚗🚗🚗
Wed.	🚗🚗🚗🚗🚗🚗🚗
Thur.	🚗🚗🚗
Fri.	🚗🚗
🚗 = 10 cars	

2 Find the totals given that ☐ = 5 cards.

a.	Joe	☐☐☐☐☐☐☐	
b.	Jenny	☐☐☐☐	
c.	James	☐☐☐☐☐☐☐☐	
d.	Jerry	☐☐☐	
e.	Jodi	☐☐☐☐☐☐	
f.	Jack	☐☐	

3 Complete the tally table.

Fruit	Tally	Total
apples	卌 卌 II	a.
pears	b.	14
bananas	c.	23
oranges	卌 卌 卌 卌 I	d.
grapes	卌 卌 IIII	e.
plums	f.	18

4 Of the people at the school carnival, how many were:

a. male? _____   b. female? _____

c. male parents? _____   d. female teachers? _____

e. students? _____   f. female students? _____

	Students	Teachers	Parents
Male	120	4	80
Female	100	6	90

5 a. What was the total number of cars parked for the week in question 1?

_____

b. Who had the most cards in question 2?

_____

c. What was the total surveyed in question 3? _____

d. What was the total number of parents at the carnival in question 4?

_____

6 In the space at the right, draw a graph showing the following information.

Pets	Number
dog	25
cat	30
rabbit	15
bird	20
fish	5
other	5

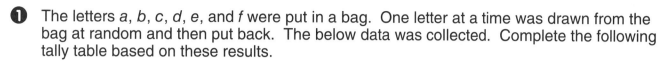

❶ The letters *a*, *b*, *c*, *d*, *e*, and *f* were put in a bag. One letter at a time was drawn from the bag at random and then put back. The below data was collected. Complete the following tally table based on these results.

a, b, c, e, f, d, e, f, c, e,

a, a, b, b, c, c, e, f, d, f,

a, a, b, b, b, c, c, b, c, b,

f, f, e, e, b, c, d, a, b, a

Letter	Tally
a	**a.**
b	**b.**
c	**c.**
d	**d.**
e	**e.**
f	**f.**

❷ Complete the following totals of the tally table.

Snack	Tally	Total
fruit	ⅲⅲ ⅲⅲ ‖	**a.**
chips	ⅲⅲ ‖	**b.**
crackers	ⅲⅲ ‖‖‖	**c.**
granola bars	‖‖	**d.**
carrots	‖‖‖	**e.**
other	ⅲⅲ	**f.**

❸ Two standard dice (1 white die and 1 gray die) were rolled several times and the below results were recorded. Using the data, complete the table.

Number of Times Each Number is Rolled					
1	2	3	4	5	6
a.	**b.**	**c.**	**d.**	**e.**	**f.**

❹ Using the data from question 3, complete the following table.

Number of Times Each Number is Rolled (Based on Color)						
Color	1	2	3	4	5	6
white	**a.**	**b.**	**d.**	2	**f.**	1
gray	2	**c.**	4	**e.**	0	2

❺ **a.** What was the total number of pieces of data collected in question 1? _____

b. What was the total number of data collected about fruit in question 2? _____

c. What was the total number of times the dice were rolled in question 3? _____

d. What was the total number of times the white die was rolled in question 4? _____

❻ Create a graph using the information from question 4.

1 The following bar graph shows the number of pies sold daily at the bakery for 5 days.

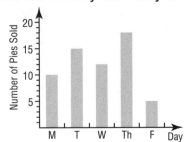

  a. What does M stand for? _____
  b. What does F stand for? _____
  c. How many pies were sold on Tuesday? _____
  d. How many pies were sold on Wednesday? _____
  e. What day were the least pies sold? _____
  f. What day were the most pies sold? _____

2 The following bar graph shows where people would travel to for vacation if they could choose one of the destinations.

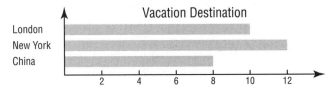

  a. What was the most popular destination? _____
  b. What was the least popular destination? _____
  c. How many people were asked? _____
  d. How many people preferred London? _____
  e. How many different locations were chosen? _____
  f. What location was preferred by less than 10 people? _____

3 Use the tally chart to complete the bar graph.

Shape	Tally
▲	ⅢⅢ Ⅰ
■	ⅢⅢ
●	ⅢⅢ ⅢⅠ
◆	Ⅲ
★	ⅠⅠ
▲	ⅠⅠⅠⅠ

  a. ▲
  b. ■
  c. ●
  d. ◆
  e. ★
  f. ▲

4 To the right is the number of books each student read for a read-a-thon. Complete the bar graph based on the tally chart.

	Student	Tally
a.	Zoe	ⅢⅢ ⅢⅢ
b.	Zack	ⅢⅢ ⅢⅢ Ⅰ
c.	Wally	ⅢⅢ ⅢⅠ
d.	Vera	ⅢⅢ ⅢⅢ ⅢⅠ
e.	Walter	ⅢⅢ ⅢⅢ Ⅰ
f.	Victor	ⅢⅢ ⅢⅠ

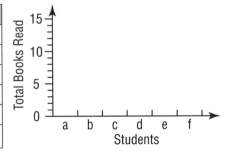

5 **a.** What was the total number of pies sold in question 1? _____

  b. What vacation destination was preferred by more than 10 people in question 2? _____

  c. What was the total number of circles in question 3? _____

  d. How many books were read altogether for the read-a-thon in question 4? _____

6 On a separate sheet of paper, create a table using the information from question 1.

Surveys and Collecting Data

1 Mark conducted a survey about people who played musical instruments. Complete his tally table.

Instrument	Tally	Total
drums	ⅢⅠ Ⅰ	a.
trumpet	ⅢⅠ ⅠⅠⅠⅠ	b.
violin	ⅢⅠ	c.
flute	d.	3
guitar	e.	7
percussion	f.	4

2 Use the information from question 1 to create a bar graph.

a. drums

b. trumpet

c. violin

d. flute

e. guitar

f. percussion

Number of People

3 Answer the following using the information in questions 1 and 2.

a. What was the most popular instrument? _____   b. What was the least popular instrument? _____

c. How many people played the guitar? _____   d. How many people played the drums? _____

e. What instrument had a total of 4 players? _____   f. What instrument had a total of 5 players? _____

4 Complete the table of collected data about colored socks.

R = red
G = green
B = blue
Y = yellow
O = orange
P = purple

R, G, B, Y, O, P, P, G,

B, Y, Y, O, P, Y, G, O,

O, P, G, R, R, R, Y, O,

G, P, G, B, B, Y, P

Color	Tally	Total

5 a. How many different instruments was data collected on in question 1? _____

b. What was the total number of people surveyed in question 1? _____

c. How many more people played the trumpet than the flute in question 1? _____

d. What were the most common colored socks in question 4? _____

6 Write 2 questions that could be asked based on the information in the table below.

	Red	Green
Boys	5	8
Girls	6	3

_____

_____

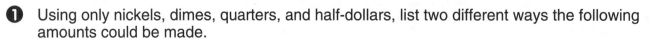

① Using only nickels, dimes, quarters, and half-dollars, list two different ways the following amounts could be made.

a. 25¢ _____ _____

b. 40¢ _____ _____

c. 50¢ _____ _____

d. 75¢ _____ _____

e. 90¢ _____ _____

f. $1.00 _____ _____

② List the different towers of blocks it is possible to make using:

a. red blocks and blue blocks, 2 blocks high. _____

_____

b. green blocks and purple blocks, 3 blocks high. _____

_____

c. yellow blocks, brown blocks, and orange blocks, 2 blocks high. _____

_____

③ Which of the following number sentences are true and which are false?

a. 27 + 14 = 14 + 26 _____

b. 83 − 23 = 26 − 83 _____

c. 11 × 12 = 6 × 2 × 11 _____

d. 9 + 6 + 5 = 5 + 5 + 10 _____

e. 33 × 2 = 33 + 33 _____

f. 888 − 88 = 800 × 1 _____

④

a. At the display, there were 6 spiders and 5 insects. How many legs were there altogether? _____

b. Tom spent the following amount of time doing homework for the week: 45 min., 30 min., 45 min., and 1 hour. How much time (in hours) did he spend doing homework altogether? _____

c. If each person at a party received $\frac{1}{4}$ of a pizza and there were 11 people at the party, how many pizzas were there? _____

⑤ Find the mistake in each of the following problems. Write the correct answers.

a.
```
  426
+318
-----
  734
```

b.
```
  671
-143
-----
  538
```

c. 5 × 20 = 10

d. 42 ÷ 6 = 5

e.
```
  1,206
+4,319
-------
  5,425
```

f.
```
  2,001
-1,463
-------
  1,538
```

⑥ Find the missing numbers to complete the magic square for 57, where every row, column, and diagonal in the square adds up to 57.

	23	
	19	
12		

Mixed Practice

1 Complete the following.

    a. 2 × 3 × 4 = _____   **b.** 2 × 5 × 7 = _____

    c. 3 × 9 × 2 = _____   **d.** 2 × 4 × 8 = _____

    e. 5 × 3 × 9 = _____   **f.** 5 × 8 × 6 = _____

2 Complete each number sentence with >, <, or = to make them true.

    a. 36 ÷ 6 ☐ 18 ÷ 3   **b.** 10 × 10 ☐ 50 × 3

    c. 60 ÷ 1 ☐ 5 × 12   **d.** 9 × 2 ☐ 36 ÷ 2

    e. 42 ÷ 6 ☐ 3 × 4   **f.** 14 − 8 ☐ 8 × 0

3 Complete the following.

    a. There are 4 hens in the pen, and each hen laid
        6 eggs this week. How many eggs are there
        altogether?   _____

    b. There are 4 cows, 3 sheep, and 7 geese. How
        many legs are there?   _____

    c. I bought two loaves of bread for $2.50 each, some
        cheese for $3.50, and an apple for 50¢. How
        much did I pay altogether?   _____

4 Fill in the missing numbers to complete the number sentences.

    a. 36 + _____ = 40   **b.** 80 − _____ = 34   **c.** _____ × 2 × 4 = 56

    d. _____ ÷ 4 = 6   **e.** 29 + _____ + 11 = 60   **f.** 50 − _____ = 19

5 **a.** Find the total of each purchase below. Which of these was more expensive?

    Purchase 1   **Purchase 2**

      $ 1.7 5   3 × $2.55 = _____

      $ 2.3 5

    + $ 1.4 5

    b. What is the difference of the two purchases? _____

6 Find the mistake in each of the following problems. Write the correct answers.

    a.   4,293   **b.**   298
        + 1,432   + 465
         5,625   663

Place Value Practice

❶ How many digits are in each of the following numerals?

    a. 407 _____   **b.** 1,265 _____

    c. 42,836 _____   **d.** 1,100 _____

    e. 145,326 _____   **f.** 102,345 _____

❷ Write each of the following as numerals.

    a. one hundred six _____   **b.** three thousand, six
                                            hundred twenty-nine _____

    c. ninety thousand, four   **d.** twenty-one thousand,
        hundred ninety-eight _____   seventy-five _____

❸ What number is:

    a. 2 more than 1,000? _____   **b.** 5 more than 989? _____

    c. 3 more than 1,099? _____   **d.** 4 more than 1,021? _____

    e. 8 more than 1,108? _____   **f.** 6 more than 1,005? _____

❹ Complete each number statement with > or <.

    a. 2,176 ☐ 2,716   **b.** 4,385 ☐ 4,835

    c. 2,110 ☐ 2,119   **d.** 7,843 ☐ 7,834

    e. 6,158 ☐ 6,185   **f.** 2,049 ☐ 2,094

❺ Write each of the following in words.

    a. 211 _____

    b. 1,340 _____

    c. 4,209 _____

    d. 762 _____

❻ Make all the different numbers possible that have a 3 in the hundreds place, using the digits 3, 7, 8, and 9.

_____

Addition and Subtraction Practice

1 Add the following.

a. 25 + 36 = _____   **b.** 34 + 50 = _____

c. 18 + 91 = _____   **d.** 89 + 38 = _____

e. 76 + 86 = _____   **f.** 37 + 46 = _____

2 Add the following.

a. 509   **b.** 361   **c.** 725
      +296   +482   +148

d. 777   **e.** 381   **f.** 188
      +185   +269   +233

3 Subtract the following.

a. 617   **b.** 504   **c.** 215
      −325   −219   −187

d. 607   **e.** 739   **f.** 866
      −452   −386   −177

4 Find the difference between:

a. 300 and 61. _____   **b.** 900 and 256. _____

c. 800 and 126. _____   **d.** 400 and 279. _____

e. 500 and 458. _____   **f.** 600 and 534. _____

5 There were 1,000 cards in a set. Leroy had collected
675 of them. How many more did he need to
complete the set?   _____

6 For a school-wide science project, 2,569 ants, 876
butterflies, and 1,362 flies were collected. How many
insects were there altogether?   _____

Multiplication and Division Practice

1 Find the product of:

    a. 9 and 6. _____   **b.** 7 and 5. _____

    c. 10 and 0. _____   **d.** 8 and 4. _____

    e. 3 and 8. _____   **f.** 6 and 2. _____

2 Fill in the missing numbers.

    a. $3 \times$ _____ $= 6 \times 5$ **b.** $5 \times 4 = 2 \times$ _____

    c. $4 \times$ _____ $= 8 \times 2$ **d.** $3 \times 4 = 6 \times$ _____

    e. $6 \times$ _____ $= 3 \times 8$ **f.** $5 \times 8 = 4 \times$ _____

3 Divide the following.

    a. $63 \div 7 =$ _____   **b.** $54 \div 6 =$ _____

    c. $48 \div 6 =$ _____   **d.** $21 \div 3 =$ _____

    e. $27 \div 9 =$ _____   **f.** $25 \div 5 =$ _____

4 Find the following. Include any remainders in your answer.

    a. 17 oranges shared by 4 teams _____

    b. 21 horses shared among 6 fields _____

    c. 22 desks in 5 rows. How many are there in each row? _____

    d. 47 days. How many weeks are there? _____

    e. 56 legs. How many spiders are there? _____

    f. 83 cards put into groups of 10. How many groups are there? _____

5 Find the product of the following prime numbers.

    a. 3 and 5 _____   **b.** 2, 3, and 5 _____

    c. 7 and 2 _____   **d.** 7, 2, and 3 _____

6 Write fourteen divided by six equals two, remainder two, as a number sentence using numerals and math symbols.

_____

Fractions Practice

1 Write *true* or *false* for each of the following statements.

a. $\frac{10}{10} = 1$ _____

b. $\frac{6}{5} = 1$ _____

c. $\frac{3}{4} = 1$ _____

d. $\frac{16}{8} = 2$ _____

e. $\frac{4}{4} = 1$ _____

f. $\frac{3}{9} = 1$ _____

2 Circle the greater fraction.

a. $\frac{1}{5}$ $\frac{1}{10}$

b. $\frac{1}{10}$ $\frac{1}{8}$

c. $\frac{1}{8}$ $\frac{1}{4}$

d. $\frac{1}{8}$ $\frac{1}{5}$

e. $\frac{1}{2}$ $\frac{1}{4}$

f. $\frac{1}{4}$ $\frac{1}{5}$

3 Complete each number line.

a.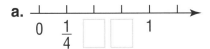

b.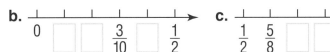

c.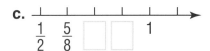

d.

e.

f.

4 Write the equivalent fraction for the following.

a. $\frac{4}{8} = \frac{\square}{2}$

b. $\frac{4}{10} = \frac{2}{\square}$

c. $\frac{1}{4} = \frac{\square}{8}$

d. $\frac{3}{4} = \frac{\square}{8}$

e. $\frac{\square}{10} = \frac{1}{2}$

f. $\frac{1}{5} = \frac{\square}{10}$

5 Order the following from greatest to least.

a. $\frac{1}{8}, \frac{1}{2}, \frac{1}{4}, \frac{3}{8}$ _____

b. $\frac{1}{10}, 1, \frac{5}{10}, \frac{9}{10}$ _____

6 Shade the squares to show $3\frac{1}{4}$.

Decimals Practice

1 Write the decimal that comes next.

    a. 0.16, 0.17, _____   **b.** 0.48, 0.49, _____

    c. 0.32, 0.33, _____   **d.** 0.20, 0.21, _____

    e. 0.55, 0.56, _____   **f.** 0.91, 0.92, _____

2 Circle the smaller decimal in each pair.

    a. 0.21   0.41   **b.** 0.60   0.50

    c. 0.29   0.16   **d.** 0.51   0.55

    e. 0.03   0.93   **f.** 0.97   0.95

3 Round each decimal to the nearest whole number.

    a. 1.46 _____   **b.** 1.79 _____

    c. 2.43 _____   **d.** 8.15 _____

    e. 9.03 _____   **f.** 4.85 _____

4 Add or subtract the following.

    a.   3.78   **b.**   5.61   **c.**   7.95

         + 2.46   − 2.35   + 1.23

    d.   4.38   **e.**   5.25   **f.**   7.90

         − 2.64   + 3.78   − 3.95

5 Order each set of decimals from least to greatest.

    a. 0.90, 0.91, 0.87, 0.85 _____

    b. 0.23, 0.45, 0.11, 0.36 _____

    c. 1.38, 1.83, 1.68, 1.36 _____

6 Find the change from eight dollars for each of the following purchases.

    a. $7.25 _____

    b. $2.29 + $1.99 _____

    c. $3.25 + $2.45 + $1.65 _____

Page 7

1. **a.** 4,364 **b.** 5,340 **c.** 5,007
2. **a.**
  b. **c.**
3. **a.** 7,372 **b.** 5,011 **c.** 2,101 **d.** 2,021
4. **a.** one thousand, two hundred seventy-five
   b. two thousand, forty-one
   c. seven thousand, nine
5. **a.** 4,003—four thousand, three
   b. 4,013—four thousand, thirteen
   c. 4,030—four thousand, thirty
   d. 4,310—four thousand, three hundred ten
   e. 4,033—four thousand, thirty-three
   f. 4,300—four thousand, three hundred
6. Possible answers: 2,367; 2,376; 2,637; 2,673; 2,736; 2,763; 3,267; 3,276; 3,627; 3,672; 3,726; 3,762

Page 8

1.

	Th	H	T	O
a.	5	0	1	0
b.	2	3	6	1
c.	6	2	0	0
d.	9	0	2	6
e.	3	1	1	1
f.	4	0	5	7

2. **a.** 1 Th 2 H 3 T 9 O **b.** 4 Th 6 H 2 T 5 O
   1 2 H 3 T 9 O 4 6 H 2 T 5 O
   1 2 3 T 9 O 4 6 2 T 5 O
   c. 8 Th 2 H 9 T 0 O
   8 2 H 9 T 0 O
   8 2 9 T 0 O
3. **a.** 300 **b.** 90 **c.** 5 **d.** 8,000
4. **a.** true **b.** false **c.** false **d.** true **e.** false **f.** false
5. **a.** 3,478 **b.** 6,099 **c.** 1,456 **d.** 2,468
6. **a.** 4,072 **b.** 4,112 **c.** 4,019 **d.** 4,090 **e.** 4,200
   f. 4,019; 4,072; 4,090; 4,112; 4,200

Page 9

1. **a.** 8,008; 8,010 **b.** 4,025; 4,030
   c. 6,087; 6,086 **d.** 3,070; 3,060
2. **a.** 2,010; 2,045; 2,076; 2,100 **b.** 1,010; 1,129; 1,147; 1,176
   c. 2,046; 4,206; 6,024; 6,402 **d.** 9,234; 9,324; 9,342; 9,432
   e. 6,006; 6,066; 6,606; 6,660 **f.** 1,428; 2,469; 3,841; 8,691
3. **a.** 1,441; 1,641 **b.** 2,048; 2,068
   c. 2,006; 5,006 **d.** 9,426; 9,456
4. **a.** 2,232; 2,220; 2,210; 2,206 **b.** 8,760; 7,860; 6,870; 6,780
   c. 4,805; 4,609; 4,503; 4,302 **d.** 1,111; 1,101; 1,011; 1,010
   e. 8,691; 7,589; 6,326; 5,245 **f.** 1,998; 1,989; 1,980; 1,976

5. 1998, 1999, 2006, 2009, 2010, 2012
6. 1,359; 1,369; 1,379; 1,389; 1,399; 1,409

Page 10

1. **a.** 4,000 **b.** 7,000 **c.** 4,000 **d.** 8,000 **e.** 2,000 **f.** 8,000
2. **a.** 7,210 **b.** 9,672 **c.** 2,029 **d.** 5,276 **e.** 6,006 **f.** 3,407
3. **a.** 3,675 **b.** 2,346 **c.** 8,832 **d.** 1,401 **e.** 4,050 **f.** 5,011
4. **a.** 4,265; 5,265 **b.** 8,050; 9,050
   c. 6,111; 7,111 **d.** 6,532; 5,532
   e. 2,781; 1,781 **f.** 4,006; 3,006
5. **a.** seven thousand, two hundred seventy-two
   b. one thousand, nine hundred fifty-three
6. **a.** two thousand, four hundred five
   b. three thousand, nineteen

Page 11

1. **a.** 1 Th 4 H 2 T 6 O **b.** 6 Th 3 H 4 T 9 O
   c. 8 Th 2 H 7 T 3 O **d.** 4 Th 2 H 0 T 1 O
2. **a.** 1,365 **b.** 4,976 **c.** 7,531 **d.** 5,067 **e.** 7,460 **f.** 872
3. **a.** tens **b.** hundreds **c.** ones **d.** thousands
4. **a.** 1,000 + 200 + 90 + 6 **b.** 5,000 + 200 + 50 + 7
   c. 9,000 + 20 + 1 **d.** 2,000 + 900 + 90 + 9
   e. 8,000 + 500 + 1 **f.** 6,000 + 700 + 90
5. **a.** 2,000 + 500 + 20 + 1 **b.** 5,000 + 70 + 8
   c. 7,000 + 100 + 1 **d.** 9,000 + 300
6.

Page 12

1. **a.** 3rd **b.** 5th **c.** 6th **d.** 8th **e.** 9th **f.** 10th
2. **a.** 1st **b.** 8th **c.** 6th **d.** 7th
3. **a.** 1st **b.** 100th **c.** 12th **d.** 21st
   e. 96th, 97th, 98th, 99th, 100th
   f. 12th, 13th, 14th, 15th, 16th
4. **a.** 3rd **b.** 5th **c.** 1st **d.** 11th **e.** 20th **f.** 50th
5. 1st, 2nd, 3rd, 4th, 5th, 6th, 7th, 8th, 9th, 10th, 11th, 12th, 13th, 14th, 15th, 16th, 17th, 18th, 19th, 20th
6. Check drawings for accuracy. 1st, 2nd, 3rd

Page 13

1. **a.** 4 × 10 **b.** 4 × 15
   double 10 = 20 double 15 = 30
   double 20 = 40 double 30 = 60
   4 × 10 = 40 4 × 15 = 60
   c. 4 × 21 **d.** 4 × 30
   double 21 = 42 double 30 = 60
   double 42 = 84 double 60 = 120
   4 × 21 = 84 4 × 30 = 120
2. **a.** 64 legs **b.** 100 legs **c.** 200 legs **d.** 160 legs
3. **a.** 25 **b.** 75 **c.** 3,000
   d. 7,500 **e.** 950 **f.** 500

4. **a.** 8 apples **b.** 150 bananas
c. 250 grapes **d.** 25 oranges
5. **a.** 200 **b.** 336
6. **a.** 20 books **b.** 35 marbles

Page 14

1. **a.** 115 **b.** 1,002 **c.** 1,020 **d.** 2,856 **e.** 3,699 **f.** 2,333
2. **a.** 596 **b.** 988 **c.** 999 **d.** 2,850 **e.** 3,757 **f.** 2,106
3. **a.** false **b.** false **c.** false **d.** false **e.** true **f.** true
4. **a.** < **b.** < **c.** > **d.** < **e.** > **f.** >
5. Answers will vary.
6. **a.** 1,411 **b.** 1,809 **c.** 2,650 **d.** Answers will vary.

Page 15

1. **a.** 26; 30 **b.** 95; 90 **c.** 54; 64
d. 424; 524 **e.** 4,426; 5,426 **f.** 2,526; 1,526
2. **a.** 100, 103, 106, 109, 112 **b.** 17, 21, 25, 29, 33
c. 100, 95, 90, 85, 80 **d.** 80, 78, 76, 74, 72
e. 3,416; 3,516; 3,616; 3,716; 3,816
f. 256, 246, 236, 226, 216
3. **a.** add 50 **b.** add 20 **c.** subtract 7
d. subtract 9 **e.** subtract 100 **f.** add 10
4. **a.** 40; 80 **b.** 581; 573 **c.** 40; 56
d. $3\frac{1}{2}$; $4\frac{1}{2}$ **e.** $1\frac{1}{2}$; $2\frac{1}{2}$ **f.** 1,566; 1,578
5. **a.** 90 **b.** 80 **c.** 100 **d.** 105
6. 100, 91, 82, 73, 64, 55, 46, 37, 28, 19 (10th term = 19)

Page 16

1. **a.** 7 tens and 9 ones **b.** 7 tens and 7 ones
c. 5 tens and 6 ones
2. **a.** 77 **b.** 94 **c.** 35 **d.** 94 **e.** 95 **f.** 88
3. **a.** 92 **b.** 69 **c.** 99 **d.** 88 **e.** 88 **f.** 97
4. **a.** 57 stickers **b.** 80 cows **c.** 43 fruits
5. **a.** 53 + 15 **b.** 23 + 37 **c.** 46 + 23 **d.** 29 + 46
6. **a.** 11 **b.** 12 **c.** 38 **d.** 68

Page 17

1. **a.** 90; 87 **b.** 100; 96 **c.** 80; 79 **d.** 80; 79
2. **a.** 797 **b.** 937 **c.** 999 **d.** 977 **e.** 995 **f.** 596
3. **a.** 170 **b.** 705 **c.** 295 **d.** 398
4. **a.** 6 5 8 **b.** 7 2 2 **c.** 4 0 3 **d.** 1 7 3
   +1 3 0   +2 4 5   +2 9 4   +2 1 5
    7 8 8   9 6 7   6 9 7   3 8 8
5. **a.** 642 **b.** 486 **c.** 826 **d.** 208
6. 428 cards

Page 18

1. **a.** 7,260 **b.** 8,849 **c.** 9,692 **d.** 5,660 **e.** 7,950 **f.** 3,850
2. **a.** 4,699 **b.** 5,796 **c.** 8,888 **d.** 7,899 **e.** 6,646 **f.** 8,997
3. **a.** 5,586 **b.** 8,478 **c.** 9,895 **d.** 4,689

4. **a.** 369 **b.** 753 **c.** 71 **d.** 244
5. 4,788 paper clips
6. 6,868

Page 19

1. **a.** 840 **b.** 861 **c.** 344 **d.** 806 **e.** 831 **f.** 421
2. **a.** 536 **b.** 902 **c.** 528 **d.** 917 **e.** 421 **f.** 952
3. **a.** 194; 311; 391; 483 **b.** 255; 536; 749; 919
4. **a.** 261 **b.** 664 **c.** 631 **d.** 900
5. **a.** 514 **b.** 586 **c.** 430 **d.** 846
6. **a.** 295 dice + 173 pencils
b. 173 pencils + 86 tops
c. 295 dice + 86 tops + 173 pencils

Page 20

1. **a.** 5,046 **b.** 7,308 **c.** 7,980 **d.** 9,794
2. **a.** 4,872 newspapers **b.** 1,360 fish
c. 5,685 lemons **d.** 6,820 sheets
3. **a.** 3,630 **b.** 7,203 **c.** 9,030 **d.** 3,702
4. **a.** 5,740 + 4,259 **b.** 8,137 + 1,862
c. 5,000 + 4,999 **d.** 7,367 + 2,632
5. $1,830
6. Word problems will vary. 1,372 + 4,685 + 3,201 = 9,258

Page 21

1. **a.** 6,921 **b.** 8,257 **c.** 7,650 **d.** 3,754
2. **a.** 6,064 **b.** 5,029 **c.** 4,982 **d.** 5,721
3. **a.** $9,175 **b.** $6,622 **c.** $6,044 **d.** $8,000
4. **a.** 734 **b.** 1,009 **c.** 1,461
d. 2,969 **e.** 4,410 **f.** 8,350
5. 387 vehicles
6. Word problems will vary.
3,250 + 1,075 + 495 + 2,860 = 7,680

Page 22

1. **a.** 500 **b.** 700 **c.** 200
d. 1,000 **e.** 3,000 **f.** 8,000
2. a, d, e (round to 4,000)
3. **a.** true **b.** false **c.** true **d.** true
4. **a.** 70 **b.** 150 **c.** 280
d. 5,130 **e.** 7,600 **f.** 2,990
5. **a.** 100 **b.** 600 **c.** 900
d. 5,600 **e.** 8,400 **f.** 6,000
6. **a.** 1,500; 2,000; 3,700; 900 **b.** 8,100 **c.** 900

Page 23

1. **a.** 35 **b.** 45 **c.** 33 **d.** 32 **e.** 24 **f.** 44
2. **a.** 35; 52; 64; 28 **b.** 33; 16; 21; 65
3. **a.** 33 **b.** 32 **c.** 14 **d.** 26 **e.** 54 **f.** 56
4. **a.** 32 sheep **b.** 11 chocolates
c. 41 cards **d.** 21 bunches

Answer Key

5. $31

6. 56 (26 ÷ 2 = 13 + 43 = 56)

Page 24

1. a.19   **b.**18   **c.**37   **d.**34   **e.**17   **f.** 58

2. a.17   **b.**18   **c.**18   **d.**27

3. a.$47   **b.**$54   **c.**$74   **d.**$13

4. a.43   **b.**25   **c.**51   **d.**56

5. a.false   **b.**false   **c.**true

6. 366 − 234 = 132

Page 25

1. a.813   **b.**911   **c.**631   **d.**174   **e.**242   **f.** 123

2. a.913   **b.**120   **c.**121   **d.**225   **e.**481   **f.** 133

3. a.$133   **b.**$233   **c.**$141   **d.**$614

4. a.
```
  156
 − 43
  113
```
b.
```
  689
 − 82
  607
```
c.
```
  399
 − 67
  332
```
d.
```
  195
 − 74
  121
```
e.
```
  732
 − 22
  710
```
f.
```
  529
 − 29
  500
```

5. a.217 bricks   **b.**311 tiles
   c.313 boys   **d.**253 stamps

6. Possible answers: less than, take away, left over, difference, minus

Page 26

1. a.326   **b.**406   **c.**45   **d.**491   **e.**238   **f.** 189

2. a.491   **b.**80   **c.**192   **d.**248   **e.**39   **f.** 102

3. a.117   **b.**608   **c.**272   **d.**389

4. a.81, 81, 142   **b.**82, 82, 245   **c.**246, 246, 475
   d.263, 263, 381   **e.**719, 719, 901   **f.** 479, 479, 800

5. a.$80   **b.**$225   **c.**$55   **d.**$33

6. one hundred seven

Page 27

1. a.1,522   **b.**1,135   **c.**1,232   **d.**2,346   **e.**2,240   **f.** 2,512

2. a.2,141   **b.**1,661   **c.**1,201   **d.**2,144

3. a.
```
  4,627
 −2,316
  2,311
```
b.
```
  7,493
 −6,243
  1,250
```
c.
```
  8,356
 −1,144
  7,212
```
d.
```
  9,852
 −6,641
  3,211
```
e.
```
  5,776
 −2,415
  3,361
```
f.
```
  8,914
 −4,302
  4,612
```

4. a.$5,000; $5,031   **b.**1,000; 1,141 marbles
   c.4,000; 4,021 cans

5. a.6,431   **b.**1,346   **c.**5,085

6. Word problems will vary. 7,959 − 3,416 = 4,543

Page 28

1. a.3,080   **b.**1,153   **c.**3,446   **d.**1,549   **e.**729   **f.** 3,478

2. a.3,699   **b.**4,779   **c.**5,158   **d.**2,685   **e.**2,204   **f.** 4,586

3. a.2,549   **b.**3,015   **c.**799   **d.**1,375

4. a.$1,265   **b.**$3,805   **c.**$2,775   **d.**$1,939

5. a.$2,524   **b.**$4,476

6. one thousand, eight hundred forty-eight

Page 29

1. a.1,290   **b.**1,760   **c.**2,370   **d.**4,920   **e.**6,210   **f.** 5,200

2. a.10 + 20 + 200 + 50 = 280
   b.50 + 100 + 200 = 350
   c.120 + 60 + 310 = 490
   d.130 + 130 + 130 + 130 = 520
   e.200 + 200 + 200 + 200 = 800
   f. 70 + 70 + 70 + 70 = 280

3. a.100 − 10 − 10 − 10 − 10 − 10 − 10 = 40
   b.200 − 30 − 30 − 30 − 30 = 80
   c.500 − 60 − 60 − 60 − 60 = 260
   d.100 − 30 − 10 − 10 = 50
   e.200 − 60 − 20 − 10 = 110
   f. 500 − 180 − 60 − 60 = 200

4. a.30 + 50 = 80   **b.**410 + 90 = 500
   c.240 + 150 = 390   **d.**300 − 60 = 240
   e.140 − 40 = 100   **f.** 520 − 110 = 410

5. a.E = 160, A = 161, D = 1   **b.**E = 380, A = 375, D = 5
   c.E = 110, A = 114, D = 4   **d.**E = 280, A = 274, D = 6

6. a.600 +200 +1,400 + 1,100 = 3,300; A = 3,311
   b.2,800 + 500 + 300 + 1,300 = 4,900; A = 4,856
   c.700 + 200 + 3,600 + 2,200 = 6,700; A = 6,667

Page 30

1. a.12   **b.**12   **c.**6; 24   **d.**5; 15   **e.**6; 0; 0   **f.** 5; 1; 5

2. a.2 × 3 = 6 or 3 × 2 = 6   **b.**5 × 4 = 20 or 4 × 5 = 20
   c.3 × 3 = 9   **d.**7 × 2 = 14 or 2 × 7 = 14

3. a.80 + 32 = 112   **b.**90 + 45 = 135
   c.60 + 18 = 78   **d.**70 + 42 = 112
   e.50 + 40 = 90   **f.** 80 + 56 = 136

4. a.double 21 = 42   **b.**double 16 = 32
   double 42 = 84   double 32 = 64
   4 × 21 = 84   4 × 16 = 64
   c.double 15 = 30   **d.**double 33 = 66
   double 30 = 60   double 66 = 132
   4 × 15 = 60   4 × 33 = 132

5. a. 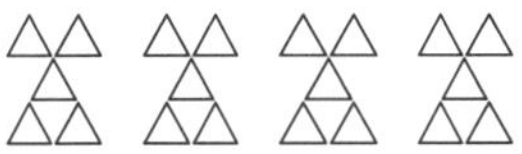 △ △ △ △ etc.   **b.**  △△△△△ etc.

6. a.176   **b.**248

Page 31

1. a.8, 4, 2, 1   **b.**50, 25
   c.80, 40, 20, 10, 5   **d.**128, 64, 32, 16, 8, 4, 2, 1

2. a.18, 36, 72, 144, 288   **b.**8, 16, 32, 64, 128
   c.10, 20, 40, 80, 160   **d.**200; 400; 800; 1,600; 3,200

©*Teacher Created Resources*   131   *#2554 Instant Math Practice*

Answer Key

3. a. true **b.** true **c.** false **d.** false **e.** true **f.** false
4. a. true **b.** true **c.** false **d.** false **e.** true **f.** false
5. answer = 566; an extra hundred was carried
6. answer = 239; should have regrouped from the tens

Page 32

1. a. 20 **b.** 80 **c.** 6 **d.** 48 **e.** 20 **f.** 56
2. a. 24 **b.** 12 **c.** 36 **d.** 22 **e.** 12 **f.** 40
3. a. 72 legs **b.** 24 legs **c.** 24 legs
　　d. 2 legs **e.** 32 legs **f.** 24 legs
4. a. 1, 2, 3, 4, 5, 6, 7, 8, 9, 10
　　b. 2, 4, 6, 8, 10, 12, 14, 16, 18, 20
　　c. 4, 8, 12, 16, 20, 24, 28, 32, 36, 40
　　d. 8, 16, 24, 32, 40, 48, 56, 64, 72, 80
5. $(5 \times 8) + (3 \times 4) + (4 \times 4) + (9 \times 2) = 40 + 12 + 16 + 18 = 86$ legs
6. $(10 \times 4) + (12 \times 2) = 40 + 24 = 64$ wheels

Page 33

1. a. 15 **b.** 100 **c.** 60 **d.** 20 **e.** 0 **f.** 70
2. a. 55 **b.** 60 **c.** 45 **d.** 110
3. a. true **b.** false **c.** true **d.** true **e.** false **f.** false
4. a. 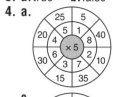 **b.**
　　c. **d.**
5. a. 5, 10, 15, 20, 25, 30, 35, 40, 45, 50
　　b. 10, 20, 30, 40, 50, 60, 70, 80, 90, 100
6. a. 20 oranges **b.** 60 granola bars

Page 34

1. a. 0 **b.** 72 **c.** 63 **d.** 30 **e.** 42 **f.** 45
2. a. 4, 2 **b.** 3, 6 **c.** 6, 36 **d.** 18, 2 **e.** 1, 3 **f.** 24, 8
3. a. 3, 27 **b.** 9, 81 **c.** 5, 45 **d.** 10, 90 **e.** 6, 54 **f.** 11, 99
4. a. $9 \times 2 = 18$ legs 　　**b.** $8 \times 6 = 48$ legs
　　c. $7 \times 3 = 21$ corners 　　**d.** $6 \times 2 = 12$ eyes
　　e. $9 \times 7 = 63$ days 　　**f.** $11 \times 3 = 33$ wheels
5. a. $27 **b.** $12 **c.** $30
6. Possible answers: $28 \times 1 = 28$; $14 \times 2 = 28$; $7 \times 4 = 28$

Page 35

1. a. 35 **b.** 72 **c.** 16 **d.** 70 **e.** 48 **f.** 27
2. a. false **b.** false **c.** true **d.** true **e.** false **f.** true
3. a. 63 **b.** 8 **c.** 45 **d.** 21 **e.** 40 **f.** 0

4. a. **b.** **c.**

d. **e.** **f.**
5. 50, 58, 66, 74, 82, 90, 98, 106, 114, 122, 130
6. 30, 37, 44, 51, 58, 65, 72, 79, 86, 93, 100

Page 36

1. a. 12 **b.** 80 **c.** 45 **d.** 40 **e.** 63 **f.** 12
2. a. 2, 4, 6, 8 **b.** 0, 7, 14, 21 **c.** 48, 56, 64, 72
　　d. 40, 45, 50, 55 **e.** 18, 21, 24, 27 **f.** 45, 54, 63, 72
3. a. 28 **b.** 48 **c.** 60 **d.** 60 **e.** 32 **f.** 16
4. a. 28, 4 **b.** 30, 5 **c.** 8, 10 **d.** 5, 10 **e.** 2, 18 **f.** 9, 6
5. a. $48 **b.** $25 **c.** $14 **d.** $36 **e.** $90 **f.** $20
6. $(6 \times 8) + (4 \times 7) = 48 + 28 = 76$ plants

Page 37

1. a. 4 **b.** 49 **c.** 25 **d.** 16 **e.** 36 **f.** 81
2. a. 1 **b.** 3 **c.** 6 **d.** 10 **e.** 15 **f.** 21
3. a. 1 **b.** 3 **c.** 6 **d.** 10 **e.** 15 **f.** 21
4. a. 3 **b.** 1 **c.** 8 **d.** 10 **e.** 5 **f.** 6
5. 55
6. a. :::: **b.**

Page 38

1. a. 10, 12, 18 **b.** 10 **c.** 12, 18
　　d. 18 **e.** 21 **f.** 12, 18, 21
2. a. false **b.** true **c.** true **d.** true **e.** false **f.** true
3. a. 3 **b.** 15 **c.** 18 **d.** 40 **e.** 24 **f.** 28
4. Possible answers:
　　a. 1, 2, 3, 4, 6, 12 **b.** 1, 2, 5, 10 **c.** 1, 5, 7, 35
　　d. 1, 7 **e.** 1, 2, 4, 8, 16 **f.** 1, 2, 4, 8, 16, 32
5. a. 15 **b.** true **c.** 24
　　d. Possible answers: 1, 2, 4, 5, 10, 20
6. 4: 4,(8,)12,(16,) 20,(24,) 28,(32,) 36,(40)
　　8:(8,)(16,)(24,)(32,)(40,) 48, 56, 64, 72, 80

Page 39

1. a. 1, 5 **b.** 1, 13 **c.** 1, 7 **d.** 1, 2 **e.** 1, 11 **f.** 1, 23
2. a. true **b.** true **c.** false **d.** false **e.** true **f.** false
3. Possible answers:
　　a. (1, 10); (2, 5) 　　**b.** (1, 20); (2, 10); (4, 5)
　　c. (1, 8); (2, 4) 　　**d.** (1, 9); (3, 3)
　　e. (1, 32); (2, 16); (4, 8) 　　**f.** (1, 4); (2, 2)

4. a. 1, 6, 2, 3   **b.** 1, 15, 3, 5
     c. 1, 20, 2, 10, 4, 5   **d.** 1, 16, 2, 8, 4
     e. 1, 12, 2, 6, 3, 4   **f.** 1, 24, 2, 12, 3, 8, 4, 6

5.

Factor	3	3	**4**	**4**	5	7
Factor	10	9	6	10	**7**	**8**
Product	**30**	**27**	24	40	35	56

6. 36: (1) 36 (2) 18 (3) 12, 4, (9) 6
     18: (1) 18 (2) 9 (3) 6

Page 40

1. a. 50 + 30 = 80
     b. 60 + 54 = 114
     c. (10 × 8) + (4 × 8) = 80 + 32 = 112

2. a. 350   **b.** 180   **c.** 480   **d.** 180   **e.** 320   **f.** 350

3. a. 2 × 70 = 140   **b.** 2 × 42 = 84
     c. 2 × 9 × 5 = 2 × 45 = 90

4. a. 70   **b.** 7   **c.** 7   **d.** 7   **e.** 9   **f.** 0

5. a. 3,200   **b.** 3,000   **c.** 2,700   **d.** 2,800

6.

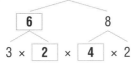

48
6   8
3 × 2 × 4 × 2

Page 41

1. a. 60   **b.** 50   **c.** 140   **d.** 180   **e.** 720   **f.** 560

2. a. 30   **b.** 90   **c.** 120   **d.** 170   **e.** 360   **f.** 230

3. a. 16 × 10 = 160   **b.** 30 × 10 = 300   **c.** 21 × 10 = 210
     d. 45 × 10 = 450   **e.** 16 × 10 = 160   **f.** 42 × 10 = 420

4. a. 360   **b.** 640   **c.** 120   **d.** 350   **e.** 300   **f.** 480

5. a. 360   **b.** 660   **c.** 500

6. 810 seats

Page 42

1. a. 12; 120; 1,200   **b.** 27; 270; 2,700
     c. 35; 350; 3,500   **d.** 90; 900; 9,000

2. a. 128   **b.** 205   **c.** 318   **d.** 390   **e.** 104   **f.** 252

3. a. 80 + 6 = 86
     b. 320 + 12 = 332
     c. (6 × 10) + (6 × 6) = 60 + 36 = 96
     d. (4 × 50) + (4 × 3) = 200 + 12 = 212

4. a. 681   **b.** 870   **c.** 896   **d.** 1,160   **e.** 785   **f.** 1,184

5. 1,008 bananas

6. Word problems will vary. 6 × 394 = 2,364

Page 43

1. a. 5, 7   **b.** 8, 9   **c.** 7, 6   **d.** 12, 4

2. a. 5   **b.** 6   **c.** 5   **d.** 8   **e.** 6   **f.** 4

3. a. 9   **b.** 5   **c.** 8   **d.** 4   **e.** 34   **f.** 32

4. a. 19   **b.** 12   **c.** 19   **d.** 13   **e.** 17   **f.** 28

5. a. 3 baskets   **b.** 5 baskets   **c.** 4 baskets
     d. 3 baskets   **e.** 7 baskets   **f.** 3 baskets

6. a. 6   **b.** 7
     c. 8 ways: 1 basket with 24 oranges
                 2 baskets with 12 oranges in each
                 3 baskets with 8 oranges in each
                 4 baskets with 6 oranges in each
                 6 baskets with 4 oranges in each
                 8 baskets with 3 oranges in each
                 12 baskets with 2 oranges in each
                 24 baskets with 1 orange in each

Page 44

1. a. 5   **b.** 10   **c.** 3   **d.** 8   **e.** 4   **f.** 8

2. a. 2 apples each   **b.** 2 slices each   **c.** 10 rows
     d. 8 rows   **e.** 2 weeks   **f.** 3 years

3. a. 15 ÷ 4 = 3 r 3   **b.** 10 ÷ 4 = 2 r 2   **c.** 24 ÷ 7 = 3 r 3
     d. 50 ÷ 6 = 8 r 2   **e.** 100 ÷ 9 = 11 r 1   **f.** 45 ÷ 7 = 6 r 3

4. a. 3 r 2   **b.** 6 r 2   **c.** 6 r 2   **d.** 10 r 2 (10 weeks, 2 days)

5. 7 spiders

6. Drawings will vary. 33 ÷ 5 = 6 r 3

Page 45

1. a. 18   **b.** 20   **c.** 49   **d.** 27   **e.** 40   **f.** 72

2. a. 4   **b.** 10   **c.** 8   **d.** 2   **e.** 5   **f.** 7

3. a. 9   **b.** 10   **c.** 8   **d.** 6   **e.** 8   **f.** 8

4. a. 3   **b.** 25   **c.** 9   **d.** 24   **e.** 4   **f.** 20

5. 7 necklaces

6. Possible drawings:
     1 row of 24 apples   2 rows of 12 apples
     3 rows of 8 apples   4 rows of 6 apples
     6 rows of 4 apples   8 rows of 3 apples
     12 rows of 2 apples

Page 46

1. a. 20   **b.** 18   **c.** 10   **d.** 12   **e.** 20   **f.** 7

2. a. 20 r 2   **b.** 18 r 2   **c.** 10 r 1   **d.** 11 r 4   **e.** 20 r 1   **f.** 6 r 5

3. a. 20   **b.** 60   **c.** 20   **d.** 35   **e.** 55   **f.** 110

4. a. 8   **b.** 14   **c.** 20   **d.** 12   **e.** 5   **f.** 12

5. a. $20   **b.** $79 ÷ 4 = $19 r 3 = $19.75

6. Estimate = 12 or 13 groups
     Number Sentence = 38 ÷ 3 = 12 r 2

Page 47

1. a. 9 r 1   **b.** 8 r 2
     2 × 9 = 18 + 1 = 19   3 × 8 = 24 + 2 = 26
     c. 9 r 2   **d.** 5 r 3
     4 × 9 = 36 + 2 = 38   5 × 5 = 25 + 3 = 28
     e. 4 r 5   **f.** 11 r 1
     6 × 4 = 24 + 5 = 29   3 × 11 = 33 + 1 = 34

2. a. 21 r 1 **b.** 11 r 1 **c.** 3 r 1 **d.** 5 r 4 **e.** 8 r 4 **f.** 14 r 1

3. a. 17 r 1 **b.** 11 r 2 **c.** 10 r 2 **d.** 11 r 1 **e.** 7 r 3 **f.** 10 r 3

4. a. 3 **b.** 6 **c.** 4 **d.** 7

5. a. 5 bottles in each row with 2 left over

b. 7 weeks and 4 days left over

c. 6 herds with 3 cows left over

d. 10 groups with 6 marbles left over

6. 4 friends; 33 ÷ 7 = 4 friends (28 books), 5 left over

Page 48

1. a. 5 r 3 **b.** 3 r 1 **c.** 2 r 1 **d.** 6 r 5 **e.** 8 r 2 **f.** 9 r 3

2. a. 5 r 3 **b.** 5 r 2 **c.** 6 r 3 **d.** 11 r 1 **e.** 20 r 1 **f.** 12 r 2

3. a. 18 **b.** 15 **c.** 17 **d.** 17 **e.** 17 **f.** 23

4. a. 10, 30, 6, 18 **b.** 8, 16, 4, 40

c. 11, 33, 11, 11 **d.** 5, 50, 100, 10

5. a. 30 r 2 **b.** 14 r 1 **c.** 10 r 4

6. 29 ÷ 6 = 4 nuggets each, with 5 left over

Page 49

1. a. 5 × 7 = 35 or 7 × 5 = 35 **b.** 3 × 10 = 30 or 10 × 3 = 30

35 ÷ 5 = 7 or 35 ÷ 7 = 5 30 ÷ 3 = 10 or 30 ÷ 10 = 3

c. 8 × 7 = 56 or 7 × 8 = 56 **d.** 9 × 8 = 72 or 8 × 9 = 72

56 ÷ 8 = 7 or 56 ÷ 7 = 8 72 ÷ 9 = 8 or 72 ÷ 8 = 9

e. 8 × 2 = 16 or 2 × 8 = 16 **f.** 4 × 1 = 4 or 1 × 4 = 4

16 ÷ 8 = 2 or 16 ÷ 2 = 8 4 ÷ 1 = 4 or 4 ÷ 4 = 1

2. a. 2 **b.** 3 **c.** 10 **d.** 4 **e.** 7 **f.** 8

3. a. 17 **b.** 24 **c.** 15 **d.** 13 **e.** 27 **f.** 12

4. a. 8 × 6 = 48 chickens **b.** 98 ÷ 7 = 14 nails

c. 5 × 9 = 45 cards **d.** 84 ÷ 7 = 12 biscuits

5. a. $12 **b.** $2

6. 20, 40, 55, 11, 10

Page 50

1. a. 60 − 21 = 39, false **b.** 75 − 18 = 57, true

c. 52 − 16 = 36, true **d.** 101 − 27 = 74, false

e. 92 − 29 = 63, true **f.** 95 − 37 = 58, true

2. a. true **b.** false **c.** false **d.** true **e.** true **f.** false

3. a. 60 ÷ 12 = 5 or 60 ÷ 5 = 12

b. 98 ÷ 14 = 7 or 98 ÷ 7 = 14

c. 48 ÷ 16 = 3 or 48 ÷ 3 = 16

d. 180 ÷ 15 = 12 or 180 ÷ 12 = 15

e. 144 ÷ 9 = 16 or 144 ÷ 16 = 9

f. 144 ÷ 18 = 8 or 144 ÷ 8 = 18

4. a. 4 × 24 = 96 or 24 × 4 = 96

b. 12 × 9 = 108 or 9 × 12 = 108

c. 13 × 6 = 78 or 6 × 13 = 78

d. 14 × 9 = 126 or 9 × 14 = 126

e. 7 × 15 = 105 or 15 × 7 = 105

f. 4 × 33 = 132 or 33 × 4 = 132

5. a. answer should be 98

b. 13 ÷ 3 ≠ 6; answer should be 44

6. 23 + __ = 37, Molly got 14 hair ribbons for her birthday.

Page 51

1. a. 7 **b.** 11 **c.** 19 **d.** $1\frac{1}{2}$ **e.** 9 **f.** $16\frac{1}{2}$

2. a. 128 **b.** 122 **c.** 130 **d.** 121 **e.** 128 **f.** 121

3. a. 179 **b.** 167 **c.** 168 **d.** 182 **e.** 178 **f.** 167

4. a. 30 **b.** 30 **c.** 24 **d.** 10 **e.** 4 **f.** 13

5. a. $5\frac{1}{2}$ **b.** $6\frac{1}{4}$ **c.** 7 **d.** $7\frac{3}{4}$

6. Check number line for accuracy.

Page 52

1. a. 1, 7 **b.** 1, 11 **c.** 1, 17 **d.** 1, 5 **e.** 1, 23 **f.** 1, 31

2. a. true **b.** false **c.** true **d.** true **e.** false **f.** false

3. a. 1, 4, 2 **b.** 1, 8, 2, 4

c. 1, 12, 2, 6, 3, 4 **d.** 1, 52, 2, 26, 4, 13

e. 1, 18, 2, 9, 3, 6 **f.** 1, 20, 2, 10, 4, 5

4. a. prime **b.** prime **c.** composite

d. composite **e.** composite **f.** prime

5. a. prime **b.** composite

6. 101, 103, 107, 109

Page 53

1. a. 20, 25, 30, 35 **b.** 50, 58, 66, 74 **c.** 5, 10, 20, 40

d. 1, 3, 9, 27 **e.** 100, 91, 82, 73 **f.** 64, 16, 4, 1

2. a. 125 **b.** 94 **c.** 32 **d.** 50 **e.** 43 **f.** 13

3. a. multiply by 5 **b.** subtract 3 **c.** multiply by 2

d. divide by 2 **e.** add 11 **f.** add 4

4. a. 13, 40, 121 **b.** 45, 445, 4,445

c. 24, 31, 38 **d.** 18, 22, 26

5. Rule: × 5 + 2; next number = 7,812

6. Answers will vary. Check patterns for accuracy.

Page 54

1. a. 107 **b.** 521 **c.** 747

d. 1,974 **e.** 19,808 **f.** 5,315

2. a. 45 **b.** 51 **c.** 25

d. 2,483 **e.** 21,260 **f.** 499

3. a. 196 **b.** 178 **c.** 292 **d.** 128 **e.** 1,042 **f.** 6,852

4. a. 296 **b.** 353 **c.** 163 **d.** 209 **e.** 764 **f.** 994

5. 10 times: 1,024; 512; 256; 128; 64; 32; 16; 8; 4; 2; 1

6. 9 times: 6; 12; 24; 48; 96; 192; 384; 768; 1,536; 3,072

Page 55

1. a. 240 **b.** 720 **c.** 490 **d.** 800 **e.** 2,100 **f.** 2,000

2. a. 180 **b.** 14 **c.** 188 **d.** 470 **e.** 160 **f.** 70

3. a. 1,029 **b.** 2,380 **c.** 2,436

d. 5,152 **e.** 4,000 **f.** 17,612

4. a. 25   **b.** 29   **c.** 47   **d.** 3   **e.** 98   **f.** 25

5. a. 392; 5,488; 76,832   **b.** 1,323; 27,783; 583,443

    c. 64; 8; 1

6. 72; 2,664; 222; 37; 7,215

Page 56

1. a. $\frac{1}{2}$ **b.** $\frac{3}{4}$ **c.** $\frac{1}{5}$ **d.** $\frac{3}{8}$ **e.** $\frac{2}{6}$ or $\frac{1}{3}$ **f.** $\frac{7}{10}$

2. a. $\frac{1}{2}$ **b.** $\frac{1}{4}$ **c.** $\frac{4}{5}$ **d.** $\frac{5}{8}$ **e.** $\frac{4}{6}$ or $\frac{2}{3}$ **f.** $\frac{3}{10}$

3. a.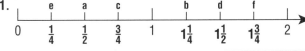

4. a. true   **b.** false   **c.** false   **d.** false   **e.** true   **f.** true

5. a. one-fourth   **b.** two-fifths   **c.** three-tenths

    d. one-eighth   **e.** one-half   **f.** three-fourths

6. a. $\frac{3}{5}$ **b.** $\frac{4}{10}$ or $\frac{2}{5}$ **c.** $\frac{4}{8}$ or $\frac{1}{2}$

Page 57

1.

    e   a   c   b   d   f

  0   $\frac{1}{4}$ $\frac{1}{2}$ $\frac{3}{4}$ 1 $1\frac{1}{4}$ $1\frac{1}{2}$ $1\frac{3}{4}$ 2

2. a.   b.   c.   d.   e.   f.

3. a. 3 circles shaded   **b.** 5 squares shaded

    c. 1 triangle shaded   **d.** 3 diamonds shaded

    e. 7 stars shaded   **f.** 7 rectangles shaded

4. a. $\frac{1}{8}, \frac{2}{8}, \frac{5}{8}, \frac{7}{8}$ **b.** $\frac{1}{5}, \frac{2}{5}, \frac{3}{5}, \frac{4}{5}$ **c.** $\frac{1}{10}, \frac{2}{10}, \frac{3}{10}, \frac{4}{10}$

5. a. $\frac{9}{10}, \frac{8}{10}, \frac{6}{10}, \frac{4}{10}$ **b.** $\frac{4}{4}, \frac{3}{4}, \frac{2}{4}, \frac{1}{4}$ **c.** $\frac{1}{2}, \frac{4}{10}, \frac{1}{5}, \frac{1}{10}$

6. a.   **b.**   **c.**

Page 58

1. a. $\frac{1}{4}$ **b.** $\frac{3}{4}$ **c.** $\frac{1}{8}$ **d.** $\frac{1}{4}$ **e.** $\frac{6}{8}$ **f.** $\frac{3}{5}$

2. a. true   **b.** false   **c.** true   **d.** false   **e.** false   **f.** true

3. a. $\frac{4}{5}, \frac{3}{5}, \frac{2}{5}, \frac{1}{5}$ **b.** $\frac{5}{8}, \frac{4}{8}, \frac{3}{8}, \frac{1}{8}$ **c.** $\frac{9}{10}, \frac{6}{10}, \frac{3}{10}, \frac{2}{10}$

4. a. $\frac{6}{10}, \frac{7}{10}, \frac{8}{10}, \frac{9}{10}$ **b.** $\frac{1}{4}, \frac{1}{2}, \frac{3}{4}, 1$ **c.** $\frac{5}{8}, \frac{6}{8}, \frac{7}{8}, 1$

5. a. $\frac{1}{10}$ **b.** $\frac{1}{5}$ **c.** $\frac{1}{2}$ **d.** $\frac{1}{8}$ **e.** $\frac{1}{4}$ **f.** $\frac{1}{10}$

6. a. one-third   **b.** $\frac{1}{4}$ $\frac{1}{3}$

Page 59

1. a. $\frac{1}{2}$ = $\boxed{\frac{2}{4}}$ **b.** $\frac{1}{2}$ = $\boxed{\frac{4}{8}}$

    c. $\frac{1}{2}$ = $\boxed{\frac{5}{10}}$ **d.** $\frac{3}{5}$ = $\boxed{\frac{6}{10}}$

    e. $\frac{4}{5}$ = $\boxed{\frac{8}{10}}$ **f.** $\frac{3}{4}$ = $\boxed{\frac{6}{8}}$

2. a. false   **b.** true   **c.** false   **d.** true   **e.** true   **f.** false

3. a. 1   **b.** 3   **c.** 5   **d.** 2   **e.** 3   **f.** 1

4. a. 2   **b.** 4   **c.** 6   **d.** 8   **e.** 10   **f.** 2

5. a. 4   **b.** 6   **c.** 2   **d.** 8

6. Possible answer:

Page 60

1. a. $1\frac{1}{2}$ **b.** $2\frac{1}{4}$ **c.** $1\frac{4}{5}$ **d.** $3\frac{3}{4}$ **e.** $1\frac{4}{10}$ or $1\frac{2}{5}$ **f.** $1\frac{5}{8}$

2. a. $1\frac{1}{2}, 2\frac{1}{2}$ **b.** $2\frac{1}{2}, 2\frac{3}{4}$ **c.** $2\frac{3}{8}, 2\frac{4}{8}$

    d. $\frac{6}{10}, \frac{7}{10}$ **e.** $1\frac{1}{4}, 1\frac{2}{4}$ **f.** $1\frac{3}{5}, 1\frac{4}{5}$

3. a. $1\frac{1}{4}$ **b.** $1\frac{5}{8}$

    c. $1\frac{7}{10}$ **d.** $1\frac{3}{5}$

    e. $1\frac{6}{8}$ **f.** $1\frac{3}{4}$

4. a. $1\frac{3}{5}$ **b.** $1\frac{9}{10}$ **c.** $2\frac{3}{4}$

5. a. $1\frac{5}{10}$ **b.** $2\frac{3}{4}$ **c.** $1\frac{8}{10}$

6. a. Check drawings for accuracy.   **b.** 29

Page 61

1. a. $\frac{45}{100}$ **b.** $\frac{76}{100}$ **c.** $\frac{51}{100}$ **d.** $\frac{27}{100}$ **e.** $\frac{95}{100}$ **f.** $\frac{33}{100}$

2. a. $\frac{55}{100}$ **b.** $\frac{24}{100}$ **c.** $\frac{49}{100}$ **d.** $\frac{73}{100}$ **e.** $\frac{5}{100}$ **f.** $\frac{67}{100}$

3. a.   **b.**   **c.**   **d.**   **e.**   **f.**

4. a. 0.05   **b.** 0.62   **c.** 0.19   **d.** 0.09   **e.** 0.40   **f.** 0.85

5.

   0.05   0.10   0.25   0.39   0.75   0.90

  0   d   f   a   c   b   e   1

6. a. 290 cents   **b.** 175 cents   **c.** 505 cents

Page 62

1. a. 0.6   **b.** 0.9   **c.** 0.4   **d.** 0.2   **e.** 0.1   **f.** 0.7

2. a. 0.3   **b.** 0.5   **c.** 0.8   **d.** 1.4   **e.** 2.1   **f.** 1.6

3. a. $1\frac{1}{10}$—1.1   **b.** $\frac{5}{10}$—0.5   **c.** $\frac{2}{10}$—0.2

    d. $\frac{10}{10}$—1   **e.** $1\frac{7}{10}$—1.7   **f.** $\frac{3}{10}$—0.3

4. a. <   **b.** =   **c.** >   **d.** <   **e.** >   **f.** =

5. a. 0.7   **b.** 0.3

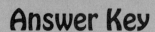

6. a. 143 cm **b.** 259 cm **c.** 850 cm

Page 63

1. a.   **b.**   **c.**

2. a. 0.56 **b.** 0.30 **c.** 0.14

3. a. 5 tenths **b.** 5 ones **c.** 5 hundredths
   d. 5 hundredths **e.** 5 tenths **f.** 5 ones

4. a. eighteen-hundredths
   b. forty-six hundredths
   c. two-hundredths
   d. thirty-hundredths or three-tenths

5. a. 0.8 **b.** 0.2 **c.** 0.4 **d.** 0.65 **e.** 0.05 **f.** 0.7

6.

Decimal	Fraction	Words	Diagram
0.4	$\frac{4}{10}$	four-tenths	
0.8	$\frac{8}{10}$	eight-tenths	

Page 64

1. a. 0.42 **b.** 0.59 **c.** 0.60 **d.** 0.78 **e.** 0.95 **f.** 0.03

2. a. 0.78 **b.** 0.75 **c.** 0.93

3. a. 0.03 **b.** 0.40 **c.** 0.17

4. a. 0.64 **b.** 0.42 **c.** 0.93 **d.** 0.01 **e.** 0.57 **f.** 0.02

5. a. 3 tenths **b.** 4 tenths **c.** 1 hundredth
   d. 3 ones **e.** 1 one **f.** 5 hundredths

6.

	H	T	O	.	Tths	Hths
a. 12.40		1	2	.	4	0
b. 613.05	6	1	3	.	0	5
c. 205.66	2	0	5	.	6	6
d. 310.95	3	1	0	.	9	5

Page 65

1. a. 0.42 **b.** 0.92 **c.** 0.66 **d.** 0.17 **e.** 0.15 **f.** 0.44

2. a. 0.13 **b.** 0.58 **c.** 0.83 **d.** 0.05 **e.** 0.79 **f.** 0.40

3. a. 0.11, 0.14, 0.16, 0.19 **b.** 0.05, 0.15, 0.45, 0.50
   c. 1.21, 1.23, 1.27, 1.28 **d.** 1.46, 1.79, 2.38, 3.66

4. a. 1 **b.** 7 **c.** 2 **d.** 3 **e.** 3 **f.** 1

5. a. 4.2 **b.** 4.6 **c.** 4.3 **d.** 4.1

6. 0.6, 0.7, 0.8, 0.9, 1.0

Page 66

1. a. 1.36 **b.** 1.19 **c.** 1.27 **d.** 1.85 **e.** 5.06 **f.** 5.90

2. a. $1\frac{60}{100}$—1.6 **b.** $1\frac{16}{100}$—1.16 **c.** $1\frac{91}{100}$—1.91
   d. $3\frac{21}{100}$—3.21 **e.** $2\frac{5}{100}$—2.05 **f.** $1\frac{50}{100}$—1.5

3. a. 1 **b.** 1 **c.** 2 **d.** 2 **e.** 2 **f.** 2

4. a. 1.31, 1.63, 1.76, 1.82
   b. 2.12, 2.22, 2.32, 2.42
   c. 14.32, 17.62, 19.63, 20.58

5. a. 1.11, 1.10, 1.08, 1.05
   b. 2.76, 2.58, 2.41, 2.39
   c. 25.91, 25.63, 25.28, 25.01

6. Check drawings for accuracy.

Page 67

1. a. 1.09—$1\frac{9}{100}$ **b.** 2.48—$2\frac{48}{100}$ **c.** 1.90—$1\frac{90}{100}$
   d. 3.96—$3\frac{96}{100}$ **e.** 1.19—$1\frac{19}{100}$ **f.** 2.84—$2\frac{84}{100}$

2. a. 0.6 **b.** 0.2 **c.** 0.49 **d.** 0.52 **e.** 1.89 **f.** 2.13

3. a. 0.8 **b.** 0.3 **c.** 0.22 **d.** 0.75 **e.** 1.09 **f.** 3.35

4. a. 0.89 **b.** 0.8 **c.** $\frac{5}{10}$

5. a. 0.26 **b.** $1\frac{1}{10}$ **c.** $\frac{17}{100}$

6. a. Sally **b.** 9 cents

Page 68

1. a. 5.9 **b.** 3.9 **c.** 2.3 **d.** 4.9 **e.** 5.5 **f.** 5.8

2. a. 7.22 **b.** 9.33 **c.** 6.27 **d.** 6.33 **e.** 5.93 **f.** 9.06

3. a. 5.49 **b.** 5.89 **c.** 8.49 **d.** 5.89

4. a. $6.61 **b.** $6.60 **c.** $6.97 **d.** $9.80 **e.** $7.94 **f.** $8.82

5. a. 6.84 **b.** 7.75 **c.** 65.06

6. 4.12 miles

Page 69

1. a. 2.48 **b.** 1.29 **c.** 0.38 **d.** 1.73 **e.** 1.69 **f.** 2.09

2. a. 1.02 **b.** 2.63 **c.** 1.22 **d.** 5.22

3. a. $2.49 **b.** $1.01 **c.** $2.73 **d.** $1.78 **e.** $2.53 **f.** $3.97

4. a. 1.14 gallons **b.** 3.14 feet
   c. 2.15 miles **d.** 2.12 pounds

5. a. $1.25 **b.** $0.75 **c.** $4.10 **d.** $0.15

6. 3.69 pounds

Page 70

1. a. 8.69 **b.** 7.91 **c.** 9.65 **d.** 4.37 **e.** 8.81 **f.** 4.41

2. a. 5.31 **b.** 5.31 **c.** 3.92 **d.** 0.55 **e.** 6.48 **f.** 4.96

3. a. 1.03 **b.** 6.98 **c.** 10.98 **d.** 0.05

4. a. 3.6 pounds **b.** $2.26 **c.** 5.56 ft.

5. 11.44

6. 3.19

Page 71

1. a. 6.5 **b.** 2.3 **c.** 4.9 **d.** 17.8 **e.** 40.7 **f.** 73.2

2. a. 17 **b.** 55 **c.** 82 **d.** 135 **e.** 569 **f.** 791

3. a. 3.9; 39 **b.** 7.1; 71 **c.** 9.5; 95
   d. 12.2; 122 **e.** 25.3; 253 **f.** 56.7; 567

4. a. 0.098 **b.** 0.025 **c.** 0.032 **d.** 0.149 **e.** 0.824 **f.** 0.666

5. a. 0.0069 **b.** 0.0034 **c.** 0.0009 **d.** 0.0788 **e.** 0.0121 **f.** 0.0472

6. a. 0.057; 0.0057 **b.** 0.091; 0.0091 **c.** 0.004; 0.0004
   d. 0.397; 0.0397 **e.** 0.507; 0.0507 **f.** 0.623; 0.0623

Page 72

1. a. 46% **b.** 39% **c.** 70% **d.** 21% **e.** 57% **f.** 3%

2. a. [grid] **b.** [grid] **c.** [grid] **d.** [grid] **e.** [grid] **f.** [grid]

3. a. 10 **b.** 8 **c.** 20 **d.** 50% **e.** 75% **f.** 90%

4. a. 50% **b.** 25% **c.** 10% **d.** 80% **e.** 63% **f.** 14%

5. 75 students were girls

6. 16% did not come

Page 73

1. a. 70% **b.** 25% **c.** 85% **d.** 90% **e.** 5% **f.** 80%

2. a. 75% **b.** 15% **c.** 100% **d.** 20% **e.** 90% **f.** 80%

3. a. 0.1—10% **b.** 0.25—25% **c.** 0.35—35%
   d. 0.75—75% **e.** 0.9—90% **f.** 0.5—50%

4. a. $\frac{60}{100}$; 60% **b.** $\frac{15}{100}$; 15% **c.** 0.35; 35%
   d. 0.7; 70% **e.** 0.22; $\frac{22}{100}$ **f.** 0.8; $\frac{8}{10}$

5. a. Level 1: 26% **b.** Level 2
   Level 2: 47%
   Level 3: 36%

6. 5 marbles

Page 74

1. a. 0.1 **b.** 0.7 **c.** 0.25 **d.** 0.14 **e.** 0.8 **f.** 0.36

2. a. 40% **b.** 30% **c.** 75% **d.** 45% **e.** 20% **f.** 63%

3. a. = **b.** = **c.** > **d.** < **e.** < **f.** =

4. a. 50%; $\frac{5}{10}$ or $\frac{1}{2}$ **b.** 10%; 0.1 **c.** 25%; $\frac{25}{100}$ or $\frac{1}{4}$
   d. $\frac{15}{100}$; 0.15 **e.** 82%; 0.82 **f.** $\frac{73}{100}$; 0.73

5. a. 10 students **b.** 4 students **c.** 5 students

6. a. 3 triangles should be shaded.
   b. 5 triangles should be circled.
   c. 2 triangles should have a smiley face inside them.

Page 75

1. a. 1 half-dollar, 1 dime, 1 nickel
   b. 2 $1 bills, 1 half-dollar, 1 quarter, 1 dime
   c. 1 $10 bill, 1 quarter
   d. 1 half-dollar, 1 quarter, 2 dimes
   e. 4 $1 bills, 1 quarter, 1 dime
   f. 1 $5 bill, 1 $1 bill, 1 half-dollar, 1 quarter

2. a. $20 bill **b.** $10 bill **c.** $5 bill
   d. $2 or $5 bill **e.** $5 bill **f.** $50 bill

3. a. yes **b.** yes **c.** yes **d.** no **e.** no **f.** no

4. a. 2 **b.** 1 **c.** 5 **d.** 20 **e.** 50 **f.** 100

5. $1.21

6. Answers will vary.

Page 76

1. a. $6.73 **b.** $9.71 **c.** $8.49 **d.** $8.43 **e.** $5.31 **f.** $8.62

2. a. $4.24 **b.** $6.49 **c.** $4.04 **d.** $5.83 **e.** $2.55 **f.** $2.58

3. a. $3.50 **b.** $2.60 **c.** $1.70 **d.** $4.45 **e.** $6.10 **f.** $2.75

4. a. $4.70 **b.** $6.50 **c.** $5.40 **d.** $5.40 **e.** $7.20 **f.** $7.90

5. $12.80

6. $9.14

Page 77

1. a. $1.25 **b.** $60 **c.** $1.20 **d.** $20 **e.** $35 **f.** $20

2. a. 40 **b.** 20 **c.** 1 **d.** 4 **e.** 10 **f.** 200

3. a. $2 **b.** 50¢ **c.** $4 **d.** $5 **e.** $10 **f.** $2.50

4. a. $4 **b.** $3 **c.** $12 **d.** $15 **e.** $40 **f.** $15

5. a. Monday = $61.15 **b.** $20.10
   Thursday = $41.05

6. Word problems will vary. $6 × 4 = $24

Page 78

1. a. 70¢ **b.** 35¢ **c.** 25¢ **d.** 40¢ **e.** 20¢ **f.** 85¢

2. a. 80¢ **b.** $0.60 **c.** $0.40 **d.** $4.00 **e.** $1.40 **f.** $8.70

3. a. $2 **b.** $2 **c.** $3 **d.** $10 **e.** $1 **f.** $4

4. a. $4.68; $4.70 **b.** $5.93; $5.95
   c. $4.48; $4.50 **d.** $3.24; $3.25

5. a. $5 + $6 + $2 = $13 **b.** $11 + $2 + $6 = $19
   c. $20 − $8 = $12 **d.** $9 − $4 = $5

6. $21 + $16 + $17 + $18 + $17 = $89

Page 79

1. a. [square] **b.** [circle] **c.** [triangle] **d.** [star] **e.** [tree] **f.** [shape]

2. a. yes **b.** yes **c.** no **d.** yes **e.** no **f.** yes

3. a. yes **b.** yes **c.** no **d.** no **e.** yes **f.** no

4. a. no **b.** yes **c.** no **d.** no **e.** yes **f.** yes

5. a. 3; 3 **b.** 4; 4 **c.** 5; 5 **d.** 6; 6

6. Check drawings for accuracy.

Page 80

1. a. 2D **b.** 3D **c.** 2D **d.** 3D **e.** 3D **f.** 2D

2. a. triangle **b.** pentagon **c.** oval
   d. parallelogram **e.** star **f.** octagon

3. Shapes a, c, and d are parallelograms and should be colored.

4. Check drawings for accuracy.

5. [semicircle drawing]

6. [octagon drawing]

Answer Key

Page 81

1. **a.** pentagon **b.** parallelogram
   c. hexagon **d.** oval
   e. octagon **f.** rhombus
2. **a.** **b.** or
   c. **d.**
3. **a.** 16 **b.** 9 **c.** 10 **d.** 24 **e.** 18 **f.** 20
4. Shapes b and e are trapezoids and should be colored.
5. Answers will vary.
6. Possible answers:
   a. 4 equal sides, 4 equal angles
   b. irregular 6-sided shape
   c. 1 curve, no edges

Page 82

1. Shapes a, c, and e are regular and should be colored.
2. **a.** square **b.** triangle **c.** pentagon
   d. hexagon **e.** octagon **f.** decagon
3. **a.** pentagon **b.** trapezoid **c.** triangle
   d. rectangle **e.** parallelogram **f.** hexagon
4. Check drawings for accuracy.
5. Answers will vary.
6. Check drawings for accuracy.

Page 83

1. **a.** yes **b.** no **c.** no **d.** yes **e.** yes **f.** no
2. **a.** yes **b.** no **c.** yes **d.** yes **e.** no **f.** yes
3. Clocks a, d, and f should be colored.
4. Possible answers:
   a. 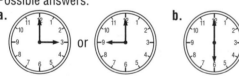 or **b.**
5. Check angles for accuracy.
6. Drawings will vary.

Page 84

1. **a.** yes **b.** yes **c.** no **d.** yes **e.** no **f.** yes
2. **a.** A **b.** C **c.** D **d.** F **e.** G **f.** F
3. **a.** yes **b.** no **c.** no **d.** no **e.** yes **f.** no
4. **a.** 5 **b.** 4 **c.** 2 **d.** 1 **e.** 6 **f.** 3
5. **a.** 3 **b.** 2 **c.** 1
6. Check angles for accuracy.

Page 85

1. **a.** no **b.** yes **c.** no **d.** no **e.** yes **f.** yes
2. **a.** **b.** **c.** **d.** **e.** **f.**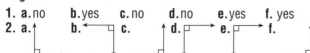

3. **a.** no **b.** no **c.** yes **d.** yes **e.** no **f.** no
4. **a.** right-angled **b.** right-angled **c.** obtuse-angled
   d. right-angled **e.** right-angled **f.** obtuse-angled
5. **a.** right **b.** obtuse **c.** acute
6.

Page 86

1. Check angles for accuracy.
2. Check angles for accuracy.
3.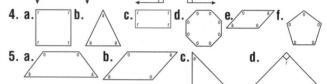
4. **a.** **b.** **c.** **d.** **e.** **f.**
5. **a.** **b.** **c.** **d.**
6. Check drawings for accuracy.

Page 87

1. **a.** 0 **b.** 1 **c.** 1 **d.** 0 **e.** 1 **f.** 3
2. **a.** yes **b.** no **c.** yes **d.** no **e.** no **f.** yes
3. **a.** no **b.** yes **c.** no **d.** yes **e.** no **f.** yes
4. **a.** **b.** **c.**
   d. **e.** **f.**
5.
6.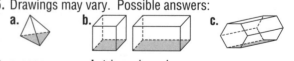

Page 88

1. **a.** cube **b.** sphere **c.** cone
   d. cylinder **e.** triangular prism **f.** pentagonal prism
2. **a.** **b.** **c.** **d.** **e.** **f.**
3. **a.** 8; 12, 6 **b.** 5; 8; 5 **c.** 4; 6; 4
   d. 8; 12; 6 **e.** 6; 9; 5 **f.** 10; 15; 7
4. **a.** **b.** **c.** **d.** **e.** **f.**
5. Drawings may vary. Possible answers:
   a. **b.** **c.**
6. **a.** cone **b.** triangular prism
   c. sphere **d.** cylinder

Answer Key

Page 89

1. Solid shapes should be duplicated.

2. Drawings may vary. Possible answers:

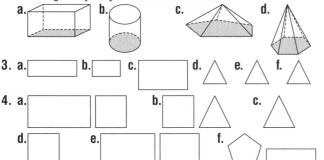

3.

4. a. b. c.
   d. e. f.

5. Drawings will vary.

6. Draw a square base and four faces as triangles meeting at one point.

Page 90

1. **a.** yes   **b.** no   **c.** yes   **d.** no   **e.** yes   **f.** yes

2. Drawings my vary. Possible answers:
   a. b. c.
   d. e. f.

3. **a.** 4   **b.** 3   **c.** 4   **d.** 3   **e.** 3   **f.** 4

4. **a.** no   **b.** yes   **c.** no   **d.** yes   **e.** yes   **f.** no

5. Drawings will vary.

6. Drawings will vary.

Page 91

1. **a.** trapezoid   **b.** pentagon   **c.** octagon
   d. rectangle   **e.** triangle   **f.** hexagon

2. **a.** 5   **b.** 6   **c.** 3   **d.** 4   **e.** 8   **f.** 4

3. **a.** 0   **b.** 2   **c.** 5   **d.** 2   **e.** 9   **f.** 20

4. a. b. c.
   d. e. f.

5. nonagon

6.

Page 92

1. **a.** yes   **b.** no   **c.** yes   **d.** no   **e.** no   **f.** yes

2. **a.** rectangles   **b.** triangles and squares
   c. pentagons and rectangles   **d.** squares and rectangles
   e. triangles and rectangles   **f.** hexagons and rectangles

---

3. **a.** 12   **b.** 9   **c.** 15   **d.** 12   **e.** 9   **f.** 18
4. **a.** 8   **b.** 6   **c.** 10   **d.** 8   **e.** 6   **f.** 12
5. **a.** rectangle   **b.** triangle   **c.** pentagon
   d. square   **e.** triangle   **f.** hexagon
6. Answers will vary.

Page 93

1. **a.** yes   **b.** no   **c.** yes   **d.** no   **e.** yes   **f.** yes
2. **a.** triangular pyramid   **b.** cone   **c.** triangular prism
   d. cylinder   **e.** sphere   **f.** square pyramid
3. **a.** 1   **b.** 1   **c.** 1   **d.** 0   **e.** 0   **f.** 0
4. **a.** 1   **b.** 2   **c.** 12   **d.** 0   **e.** 12   **f.** 9
5. **a.** 1   **b.** 2   **c.** 6   **d.** 0   **e.** 6   **f.** 5
6.

Page 94

1. **a.** yes   **b.** no   **c.** yes   **d.** no   **e.** no   **f.** yes
2. **a.** v = 6; e = 10   **b.** v = 5; e = 8   **c.** v = 5; e = 8
   d. v = 7; e = 12   **e.** v = 4; e = 6   **f.** v = 9; e = 16
3. a. b. c.

   d. e. f.
4. **a.** square   **b.** rectangle   **c.** triangle
   d. pentagon   **e.** octagon   **f.** hexagon
5. **a.** square pyramid   **b.** rectangular pyramid
   c. triangular pyramid   **d.** pentagonal pyramid
   e. octagonal pyramid   **f.** hexagonal pyramid
6. **a.** square   **b.** triangle

Page 95

1. a.
   b.
   c.
   d.
   e.
   f.
   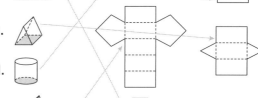 

2. **a.** yes   **b.** yes   **c.** no   **d.** yes   **e.** no   **f.** yes
3. **a.** cube   **b.** triangular prism
   c. triangular prism   **d.** triangular pyramid
   e. triangular pyramid   **f.** square pyramid

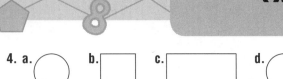

Answer Key

4. a. **b.** **c.** **d.**

5. square pyramid

6.

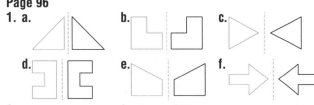

Page 96

1. a. 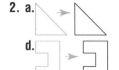 **b.** **c.**

d.  **e.** **f.**

2. a. **b.** **c.**

d. **e.** **f.**

3. a. **b.** **c.**

d. **e.** **f.**

4. a. reflect **b.** rotate **c.** translate
d. rotate **e.** reflect **f.** translate

5.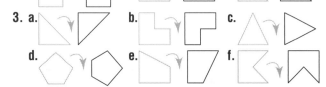

6.

Page 97

1. a. yes **b.** yes **c.** no **d.** no **e.** yes **f.** yes
2. a. yes **b.** yes **c.** no **d.** no **e.** yes **f.** yes
3. a. **b.** **c.** **d.**
4. a. **b.** **c.** **d.**

5. Drawings will vary.
6. Drawings will vary.

Page 98

1. a. lion **b.** elephant **c.** bear
d. tiger **e.** horse **f.** elephant
2. a. glue **b.** pencils **c.** markers
d. rubber bands **e.** paper clips **f.** staples

3. a.–e.

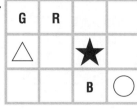

f. middle row, 3 from the left OR middle row, 2 from the right
4. a. middle of front row **b.** front row, left corner
c. front row, second from right **d.** front row, second from left
e. back row, left corner **f.** back row, middle
5. a. tiger **b.** pencils
c. Square should be drawn in the box to the right of the star.
d. front row, right corner

6.

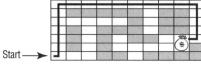

Move up 6 spaces, right 9 spaces, down 4 spaces, then left 1 space.

Page 99

1. a. S **b.** E **c.** NE **d.** SE **e.** W **f.** NW
2. a. boat **b.** mountains **c.** tree
d. park **e.** school **f.** house
3. a. east **b.** southeast **c.** north
d. west **e.** northeast **f.** northwest

4.

5.

6. a. north **b.** northeast **c.** northwest

Page 100

1. a. pentagon **b.** square **c.** triangle
d. trapezoid **e.** rectangle **f.** circle

2.

3. a. (B, 4) **b.** (D, 4) **c.** (B, 2) **d.** (D, 2) **e.** (B, 0) **f.** (D, 0)

4.

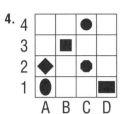

5. (D, 2)

6. Answers will vary.

Page 101

1. a. (B, 4)   **b.** (A, 3)   **c.** (A, 1)   **d.** (D, 5)   **e.** (D, 3)   **f.** (C, 1)

2. a. dog   **b.** duck   **c.** bird

   d. butterfly   **e.** pig   **f.** fish

3. a. (B, 2)   **b.** (D, 1)   **c.** (C, 4)   **d.** (A, 1)   **e.** (B, 1)   **f.** (A, 2)

4.

5. a. (D, 4)   **b.** lamb   **c.** (A, 4)

   d. Half circle should be drawn in (D,4).

6. Question 1: (A, 2), (B, 1), (B, 3), (B, 5), (C, 2), (C, 4), (D, 1)
   Question 3: (A, 3), (C, 3)

Page 102

1. a.
8	1	6
3	5	7
4	9	2

b.
3	8	7
10	6	2
5	4	9

c.
6	11	4
5	7	9
10	3	8

d.
15	1	11
5	9	13
7	17	3

e.
11	34	24
36	23	10
22	12	35

f.
71	89	17
5	59	113
101	29	47

2. a.   **b.**   **c.**   **d.**

(and)

3. a. 5   **b.** 9   **c.** 27   **d.** 20

4. a. rotation   **b.** reflection

   c. translation or reflection   **d.** translation

   e. rotation   **f.** rotation

5. 4,589 = Mystery Number

6. Answers will vary.

Page 103

1. a. yes   **b.** yes   **c.** yes   **d.** no   **e.** yes   **f.** yes

2. a. triangle   **b.** parallelogram   **c.** triangle

   d. triangle   **e.** square   **f.** square

3. a. triangle   **b.** triangle   **c.** square

   d. triangle   **e.** parallelogram   **f.** triangle

4. a. false   **b.** true   **c.** false   **d.** true   **e.** true   **f.** true

5.

6. Check paper folding for accuracy.

Page 104

1. a. 6 min. past 8:00 or 8:06   **b.** 9 min. to 9:00 or 8:51

   c. 16 min. past 6:00 or 6:16   **d.** 24 min. to 7:00 or 6:36

   e. 11 min. past 2:00 or 2:11   **f.** 4 min. to 10:00 or 9:56

2. a. 5 minutes   **b.** 10 minutes   **c.** 15 minutes

   d. 30 minutes   **e.** 40 minutes   **f.** 55 minutes

3. a. 15 min. to 6:00   **b.** 20 min. to 5:00

   c. 25 min. to 1:00   **d.** 10 min. past 12:00

   e. 25 min. past 10:00   **f.** 20 min. past 4:00

4. a.   **b.**   **c.**

   d.   **e.**   **f.**

5. a. 7:15; quarter past 7   **b.** 8:45; quarter to 9

   c. 6:30; half past 6   **d.** 6:00; six o'clock

   e. 2:55; 5 min. to 3

6.

Page 105

1. a. <   **b.** <   **c.** >   **d.** >   **e.** <   **f.** >

2. a. 17 past 4   **b.** 11 to 7   **c.** 29 past 8

   d. 4 to 11   **e.** 35 past 7   **f.** 25 to 2

3. a.   **b.**   **c.**

   d.   **e.**   **f.**

4. a. 17 minutes   **b.** 16 minutes   **c.** 54 minutes

   d. 3 minutes   **e.** 25 minutes   **f.** 4 minutes

5. a.   **b.**   **c.**

   7:15   2:30   7:45

d.  **e.**   **f.**

6. 6 hours 30 minutes

Page 106

1. a. 1   **b.** 120   **c.** 12   **d.** 14   **e.** 24   **f.** 3

2. a. May   **b.** August   **c.** September
   d. November   **e.** March   **f.** January

3. a. February   **b.** Monday   **c.** Wednesday
   d. December   **e.** January   **f.** September

4. a. Sunday   **b.** Saturday   **c.** Tuesday
   d. Thursday   **e.** Wednesday   **f.** Friday

5. a. 7   **b.** 13   **c.** 15   **d.** 16   **e.** 21   **f.** 4

6. a. March 1   **b.** March 26   **c.** March 6
   d. March 31   **e.** March 14   **f.** March 23

Page 107

1. a. 7:30   **b.** 11:00   **c.** 8:30   **d.** 9:30   **e.** 6:30   **f.** 9:00

2.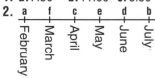

3. a. 7:40   **b.** 7:55   **c.** 8:40   **d.** 7:20   **e.** 8:15   **f.** 7:10

4. a. Swimming Hole   **b.** Football St.   **c.** Basketball Rd.
   d. Cricket Rd.   **e.** Ballet Bend   **f.** Hockey St.

5. a. 8:00   **b.** 8:25   **c.** Running Ln.

6. a. 7:40   **b.** 8:25

Page 108

1. a. 12   **b.** 3   **c.** 36   **d.** true

2. a. A = 7 cm   **b.** A = 5 cm   **c.** A = 2 in.
   d. A = 3 in.   **e.** A = 1 in.   **f.** A = 4 in.

3. Check lines for accuracy.

4. a. in.   **b.** ft.   **c.** cm   **d.** in.   **e.** ft.   **f.** in. or cm

5. Answers will vary.

6. Answers will vary.

Page 109

1. a. 9.5 cm   **b.** 6.25 in.   **c.** 2.75 in.   **d.** 10.5 ft.

2. a. <   **b.** >   **c.** >   **d.** >   **e.** <   **f.** >

3. a. 9.5 cm   **b.** 4.5 in.   **c.** 2.75 in.
   d. 6.5 cm   **e.** 3.25 in.   **f.** 2.5 in.

4. Check lines for accuracy.

5. a. 6   **b.** 4   **c.** 1   **d.** 3   **e.** 5   **f.** 2

6. 25.4 ft.

Page 110

1. a. P = 2 in. + 5 in. + 2 in. + 5 in. = 14 in.
   b. P = 3 in. + 4 in. + 5 in. = 12 in.
   c. P = 2 ft. + 4 ft. + 1 ft. + 2 ft. + 1 ft. + 2 ft. = 12 ft.
   d. P = 10 ft. + 9 ft. + 6 ft. + 7 ft. = 32 ft.

2. a. 21 ft.   **b.** 12 in.   **c.** 16 cm   **d.** 32 in.

3. a. 26 cm   **b.** 38 in.   **c.** 70 ft.   **d.** 76 ft.

4. a. 28 in.   **b.** 15 in.   **c.** 10 ft.   **d.** 36 in.

5. 36 ft.

6. Check drawings for accuracy.

Page 111

1. a. 6 units^2 **b.** 7 units^2 **c.** 5 units^2
   d. 6 units^2 **e.** 8 units^2 **f.** 6 units^2

2. a. 7 units^2 **b.** 5 units^2 **c.** 14 units^2 **d.** 12 units^2

3. a. ft.^{2} **b.** in.^{2} **c.** ft.^{2} **d.** ft.^{2} **e.** ft.^{2} **f.** in.^{2}

4. a. 12 cm^2 **b.** 25 ft.^{2} **c.** 54 in.^{2} **d.** 49 in.^{2}

5. a. 40 in.^{2} **b.** 108 in.^{2} **c.** 88 in.^{2} **d.** 21 in.^{2}

6. a. 10 cm^2 **b.** 30 in.^{2}

Page 112

1. a. 15 cm^2 **b.** 49 m^2 **c.** 87 in.^{2} **d.** 35 ft.^{2} **e.** 74 yd.^{2}

2. a. >   **b.** <   **c.** <   **d.** <

3. a. 6 units^2 **b.** 5 units^2 **c.** 10 units^2
   d. 6 units^2 **e.** 8 units^2 **f.** 6 units^2

4. a. 10 units   **b.** 12 units   **c.** 14 units
   d. 14 units   **e.** 14 units   **f.** 12 units

5. Check drawings for accuracy.

6. Check drawings for accuracy.

Page 113

1. a. 40 lb.   **b.** 20 lb.   **c.** 100 lb.   **d.** 64 lb.   **e.** 18 lb.   **f.** 96 lb.

2. a. 1   **b.** 2   **c.** 3   **d.** 5   **e.** 6   **f.** 4

3. a. lb.   **b.** lb.   **c.** oz.   **d.** lb.   **e.** oz.   **f.** oz.

4. a. 8 oz.   **b.** 12 oz.   **c.** 4 oz.   **d.** 24 oz.

5. 2 grapefruits

6. a. 11 oz.   **b.** 8 oz.

Page 114

1. a. yes   **b.** no   **c.** no   **d.** yes   **e.** yes   **f.** no

2. a. 6   **b.** 4   **c.** 3   **d.** 4

3. a. red   **b.** yes   **c.** yes   **d.** yes   **e.** yes   **f.** no

4. a. yes   **b.** no   **c.** yes   **d.** no   **e.** yes   **f.** no

5. 1, 3, 5   1, 5, 3   3, 1, 5   3, 5, 1   5, 1, 3   5, 3, 1

6. 6 possible sock pairs: RG, RB, RY, GB, GY, BY

Page 115

1. a. yellow   b. blue   c. yes

   d. no   e. no   f. green and orange

2. a. $\frac{4}{4}$ or 1; certain   b. $\frac{2}{4}$ or $\frac{1}{2}$ c. 0; impossible

   d. $\frac{2}{4}$ or $\frac{1}{2}$ e. $\frac{2}{4}$ or $\frac{1}{2}$ f. $\frac{2}{4}$ or $\frac{1}{2}$

3. a. unlikely   b. certain   c. equal chance

   d. equal chance   e. likely   f. impossible

4. a. true   b. false   c. true   d. false   e. true   f. false

5. a. false   b. true   c. false   d. true   e. false   f. false

6. a. yes   b. yes   c. yes   d. yes   e. yes   f. no

Page 116

1. a. 50   b. 20   c. 40   d. 20   e. 130   f. 10 houses

2. a. 1:00–2:00   b. 11:00–12:00

   c. 9:00–10:00   d. 10:00–11:00 and 12:00–1:00

   e. 11:00–12:00 and 1:00–2:00   f. 9:00–10:00

3. a. basketball   b. volleyball

   c. football and soccer   d. 4 students

   e. softball   f. yes

4.

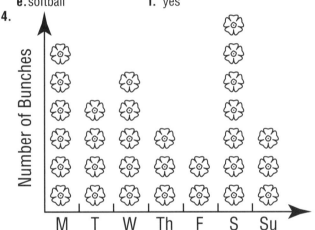

5. a. gray   b. 45 computers   c. 9 students   d. 30 bunches

6. Check graph for accuracy.

Page 117

1. a. 40   b. 19   c. 21   d. $\frac{19}{40}$ e. $\frac{21}{40}$ f. $\frac{21}{40}$

2. a. JHT   b. I   c. JHT III   d. JHT II   e. JHT   f. IIII

3. a. 30   b. football

   c. swimming   d. tennis and basketball

   e. 2   f. 12

4. a. water   b. milk   c. 3   d. 2   e. water   f. juice

5. a. 9   b. 15   c. JHT JHT II; 12   d. III; 3   e. JHT I   f. JHT IIII

6. Check tally table for accuracy.

Page 118

1. a. 30   b. 30   c. 50   d. Mon. and Wed.   e. Friday   f. 30

2. a. 35   b. 25   c. 40   d. 20   e. 30   f. 15

3. a. 12   b. JHT JHT IIII   c. JHT JHT JHT JHT III

   d. 21   e. 14   f. JHT JHT JHT III

4. a. 204   b. 196   c. 80   d. 6   e. 220   f. 100

5. a. 200   b. James   c. 102   d. 170

6. Check graph for accuracy.

Page 119

1. a. JHT II   b. JHT JHT   c. JHT III

   d. III   e. JHT I   f. JHT I

2. a. 12   b. 7   c. 9   d. 3   e. 4   f. 5

3. a. 5   b. 4   c. 6   d. 4   e. 2   f. 3

4. a. 3   b. 3   c. 1   d. 2   e. 2   f. 2

5. a. 40   b. 40   c. 24   d. 13

6. Check graph for accuracy.

Page 120

1. a. Monday   b. Friday   c. 15

   d. 12   e. Friday   f. Thursday

2. a. New York   b. China   c. 30

   d. 10   e. 3   f. China

3.

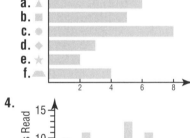

4.

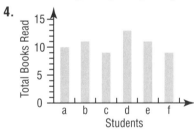

5. a. 60   b. New York   c. 8   d. 63

6.

Day	Pies Sold
Mon.	10
Tue.	15
Wed.	12
Thu.	18
Fri.	5

Page 121

1. a. 6   b. 9   c. 5   d. III   e. JHT II   f. IIII

2.

3. **a.** trumpet   **b.** flute   **c.** 7
    d. 6   **e.** percussion   **f.** violin

4.

Color	Tally	Total
red	IIII	4
green	HHII I	6
blue	IIII	4
yellow	HHII I	6
orange	HHII	5
purple	HHII I	6

5. **a.** 6   **b.** 34   **c.** 6   **d.** green, yellow, and purple

6. Answers will vary.

Page 122

1. Answers will vary.

2. **a.** RR, RB, BB, BR
    b. GGG, GGP, GPG, GPP, PPP, PPG, PGP, PGG
    c. YY, YB, YO, BB, BY, BO, OO, OY, OB

3. **a.** false   **b.** false   **c.** true   **d.** true   **e.** true   **f.** true

4. **a.** 78 legs   **b.** 180 min. = 3 hours   **c.** 3 pizzas

5. **a.** answer = 744   **b.** answer = 528   **c.** answer = 100
    d. answer = 7   **e.** answer = 5,525   **f.** answer = 538

6.

8	23	26
37	19	1
12	15	30

Page 123

1. **a.** 24   **b.** 70   **c.** 54   **d.** 64   **e.** 135   **f.** 240

2. **a.** =   **b.** <   **c.** =   **d.** =   **e.** <   **f.** >

3. **a.** 24 eggs   **b.** 42 legs   **c.** $9

4. **a.** 4   **b.** 46   **c.** 7   **d.** 24   **e.** 20   **f.** 31

5. **a.** Purchase 1 = $5.55   Purchase 2 = $7.65 (more)
    b. $2.10

6. **a.** answer = 5,725   **b.** answer = 763

Page 124

1. **a.** 3   **b.** 4   **c.** 5   **d.** 4   **e.** 6   **f.** 6

2. **a.** 106   **b.** 3,629   **c.** 90,498   **d.** 21,075

3. **a.** 1,002   **b.** 994   **c.** 1,102   **d.** 1,025   **e.** 1,116   **f.** 1,011

4. **a.** <   **b.** <   **c.** <   **d.** >   **e.** <   **f.** <

5. **a.** two hundred eleven
    b. one thousand, three hundred forty
    c. four thousand, two hundred nine
    d. seven hundred sixty-two

6. 7,389; 7,398; 8,379; 8,397; 9,378; 9,387

Page 125

1. **a.** 61   **b.** 84   **c.** 109   **d.** 127   **e.** 162   **f.** 83

2. **a.** 805   **b.** 843   **c.** 873   **d.** 962   **e.** 650   **f.** 421

3. **a.** 292   **b.** 285   **c.** 28   **d.** 155   **e.** 353   **f.** 689

4. **a.** 239   **b.** 644   **c.** 674   **d.** 121   **e.** 42   **f.** 66

5. 325 cards

6. 4,807 insects

Page 126

1. **a.** 54   **b.** 35   **c.** 0   **d.** 32   **e.** 24   **f.** 12

2. **a.** 10   **b.** 10   **c.** 4   **d.** 2   **e.** 4   **f.** 10

3. **a.** 9   **b.** 9   **c.** 8   **d.** 7   **e.** 3   **f.** 5

4. **a.** 4 oranges per team and 1 left over
    b. 3 horses in each field and 3 left over
    c. 4 desks in each row and 2 left over
    d. 6 weeks and 5 days
    e. 7 spiders
    f. 8 groups and 3 cards left over

5. **a.** 15   **b.** 30   **c.** 14   **d.** 42

6. $14 \div 6 = 2 \text{ r } 2$

Page 127

1. **a.** true   **b.** false   **c.** false   **d.** true   **e.** true   **f.** false

2. **a.** $\frac{1}{5}$ **b.** $\frac{1}{8}$ **c.** $\frac{1}{4}$ **d.** $\frac{1}{5}$ **e.** $\frac{1}{2}$ **f.** $\frac{1}{4}$

3. **a.** $\frac{1}{2}$ (or $\frac{2}{4}$); $\frac{3}{4}$ **b.** $\frac{1}{10}$; $\frac{2}{10}$ (or $\frac{1}{5}$); $\frac{4}{10}$ (or $\frac{2}{5}$)
    c. $\frac{6}{8}$ (or $\frac{3}{4}$); $\frac{7}{8}$ **d.** $\frac{2}{5}$; $\frac{3}{5}$; $\frac{4}{5}$; 1 (or $\frac{5}{5}$)
    e. $\frac{6}{10}$ (or $\frac{3}{5}$); $\frac{8}{10}$ (or $\frac{4}{5}$); $\frac{9}{10}$ **f.** $\frac{1}{6}$; $\frac{2}{6}$ (or $\frac{1}{3}$), $\frac{5}{6}$

4. **a.** 1   **b.** 5   **c.** 2   **d.** 6   **e.** 5   **f.** 2

5. **a.** $\frac{1}{2}, \frac{3}{8}, \frac{1}{4}, \frac{1}{8}$
    b. 1, $\frac{9}{10}, \frac{5}{10}, \frac{1}{10}$

6.

Page 128

1. **a.** 0.18   **b.** 0.50   **c.** 0.34   **d.** 0.22   **e.** 0.57   **f.** 0.93

2. **a.** 0.21   **b.** 0.50   **c.** 0.16   **d.** 0.51   **e.** 0.03   **f.** 0.95

3. **a.** 1   **b.** 2   **c.** 2   **d.** 8   **e.** 9   **f.** 5

4. **a.** 6.24   **b.** 3.26   **c.** 9.18   **d.** 1.74   **e.** 9.03   **f.** 3.95

5. **a.** 0.85, 0.87, 0.90, 0.91   **b.** 0.11, 0.23, 0.36, 0.45
    c. 1.36, 1.38, 1.68, 1.83

6. **a.** $8.00 − $7.25 = $0.75
    b. $8.00 − $4.28 = $3.72
    c. $8.00 − $7.35 = $0.65